ABIDING IN GRACE

DAILY REFLECTIONS ON MANIFESTING GOD'S LOVE

A Devotion To Aid And Strengthen Your Christian Faith

Osvaldo R Burgos JR

Copyright

TABLE OF CONTENTS

FAITH 2
HOPE 14
LOVE 26
GRACE 38
WISDOM 50
DISCERNMENT 62
RENEWAL 74
TRANSFORMATION 86
SPIRITUAL DISCIPLINE 98
SELF-CONTROL 110
PEACE 122
JOY 134
FORGIVENESS 146
HUMILITY 158
PATIENCE 170
FAITHFULNESS 182
KINDNESS 194
GENTLENESS 206
GRATITUDE 218
TRUST 230

FAITH

THE FOUNDATION OF FAITH

"Now faith is confidence in what we hope for and assurance about what we do not see."

Bible Verse: Hebrews 11:1 (NIV)

Faith is not merely an intellectual agreement with certain facts about God; it is a deep, personal trust in His character and promises. The Bible tells us that faith is "confidence in what we hope for" it assures us of things yet to come. It's not a vague wish or uncertainty but a solid belief in God's ability to fulfill His promises. Faith is also "assurance about what we do not see," meaning we trust in God's work even when it's invisible to us. Faith serves as the foundation of our relationship with God, replacing doubt with trust and uncertainty with confidence in His faithfulness.

Think about the promises of God that you are holding onto right now. How does faith change your perspective on the challenges you're facing? Faith assures us that even when things appear uncertain or out of control, God is still faithful in keeping His word. Reflect on a situation where you trusted God for something you couldn't yet see and how He proved His faithfulness.

PRAYER

Heavenly Father, thank You for the gift of faith. I choose to trust in your promises, even when I cannot see the outcome. Help me to stand firm on the foundation of faith and to be confident in your ability to fulfill every promise you've made. Strengthen my faith each day and teach me to lean on you in all circumstances. In Jesus' name, Amen.

FAITH DURING TIMES OF TROUBLES

"Consider it pure joy, my brothers and sisters, whenever you face trials of many kinds because you know that the testing of your faith produces perseverance."

Bible Verse: James 1:2-3 (NIV)

Faith is not something that flourishes only in times of peace; it is often refined and made stronger in the crucible of trials. The testing of our faith doesn't mean that God is trying to punish us; rather, He is using the trials to shape our character and make us more steadfast. Trials help to refine our faith, stripping away the surface level of trust and revealing the depth of our commitment to God. Through difficulties, our faith becomes more resilient, producing the kind of perseverance that helps us endure, grow, and bring glory to God.

Consider the trials you are currently facing or have faced in the past. How have they shaped your faith? Rather than seeing hardships as obstacles, try to view them as opportunities for God to strengthen your faith. What can you learn from these moments that will deepen your trust in Him?

PRAYER

Lord, when trials come my way, help me to count them as joy, knowing that they are refining my faith. I ask for the strength to remain steadfast in the midst of difficulty and to trust you even when circumstances are hard. May my faith grow stronger through every challenge, and may I bring glory to you through my perseverance. In Jesus' name, Amen.

FAITH IN GOD'S PROVISION

"And my God will meet all your needs according to the riches of his glory in Christ Jesus."

Bible Verse: Philippians 4:19 (NIV)

Faith in God's provision is more than a belief that God can provide for us; it is an assurance that He will. God's provision is not limited to material wealth or physical needs but extends to emotional, spiritual, and relational needs as well. He knows what we need even before we ask, and His provision is always perfectly timed and perfectly suited to our lives. When we put our trust in His ability to supply, we shift our focus from worrying about our circumstances to trusting in His faithfulness and goodness. Faith in God's provision means learning to rely on Him in every situation, trusting that He will meet our needs according to His perfect will.

Reflect on times when God has provided for you in unexpected ways. How did that strengthen your faith? When you face future uncertainties, how can you lean more into God's promises of provision? Trusting in God's provision requires us to surrender our anxieties and believe that He knows exactly what we need.

PRAYER

Father, thank You for being a God who provides. Help me to trust you fully with my needs, whether big or small. Teach me to rely on your perfect timing and provision and to find peace in knowing that you will supply every need. Strengthen my faith in your ability to provide for me in every area of my life. In Jesus' name, Amen.

GROWING FAITH

"Consequently, faith comes from hearing the message, and the message is heard through the word about Christ."

Bible Verse: Romans 10:17 (NIV)

Faith is not something we must muster up on our own; it grows as we actively seek to know God through His Word. The more we hear the Word of God, the more our faith is nurtured and deepened. It is through listening and understanding the promises in Scripture that we learn to trust God more fully. A faith that is rooted in the knowledge of God's Word is a faith that can withstand any storm. God's word is the primary means by which we grow in faith, and as we immerse ourselves in it, we gain a clearer understanding of His character, His faithfulness, and His promises.

How much time do you spend reading and reflecting on God's Word? What is one area of your life where you need to grow in faith? Spend time in the Bible this week, allowing God's truth to speak to you and build your trust in Him. Reflect on the specific promises of God that speak to your current situation.

PRAYER

Lord, help me to grow in faith through Your Word. Open my eyes to the truths You want me to see, and help me to trust in Your promises more deeply. May Your Word be a lamp to my feet, guiding me and strengthening my faith every day. In Jesus' name, Amen.

LIVING BY FAITH

"For we live by faith, not by sight."

Bible Verse: 2 Corinthians 5:7 (NIV)

Living by faith is not about acknowledging what God can do but choosing to act on what we believe about Him. It requires us to trust in God's direction even when we cannot see the full picture. Faith involves making decisions that reflect our trust in God's guidance, even when the path ahead is unclear. To walk by faith means to live our everyday lives with unwavering confidence in God's plan, regardless of our circumstances or what we can perceive with our physical senses. It's about relying on God to lead us, even when we cannot predict the outcome.

What decisions are you currently facing that require you to walk by faith? How can you take steps of obedience, trusting God even though you cannot see the full outcome? Living by faith requires a willingness to surrender control and follow where God leads, even when it feels uncertain.

PRAYER

God, teach me to walk by faith and not by sight. Help me to trust You with every decision and every step I take, knowing that You are guiding me. When I face uncertainty, give me the courage to follow You and to rest in the assurance that You are in control. In Jesus' name, Amen.

HOPE

THE SOURCE OF OUR HOPE

"May the God of hope fill you with all joy and peace as you trust in him, so that you may overflow with hope by the power of the Holy Spirit."

Bible Verse: Romans 15:13 (NIV)

Hope is not just a fleeting wish or desire but a confident expectation that is grounded in God's nature and promises. Our hope doesn't come from the circumstances around us but from the unchanging God, who is the source of all hope. As we trust in Him, He fills us with joy and peace, even in the midst of life's challenges. The Holy Spirit empowers us to overflow with hope, enabling us to live with confidence and peace despite what's going on around us. Hope is not a passive waiting but an active, powerful expectation of God's goodness.

Where are you finding your hope today? Is it anchored in God's promises or temporary circumstances? Remember, true hope comes from trusting in God's ability to bring good out of every situation. Reflect on how God has been faithful in bringing hope into your life, even in tough times.

PRAYER

God of all hope, thank you for being the source of my hope. Fill me with your joy and peace as I trust in You. May Your Holy Spirit overflow in my heart, empowering me to live with confident hope, no matter what I face. In Jesus' name, Amen.

HOPE IN THE WAITING

"The Lord is good to those whose hope is in him, to the one who seeks him; it is good to wait quietly for the salvation of the Lord."

Bible Verse: Lamentations 3:25-26 (NIV)

Waiting is often the hardest part of the journey, especially when we are unsure of how long we will have to wait or when the answer will come. But in the waiting, hope is cultivated. The Lord is good to those who place their hope in Him and wait patiently for His timing. This passage reminds us that there is goodness in the waiting, as it is during this time that God refines our hearts, teaches us to trust Him more fully, and prepares us for what is ahead. Hope grows in our hearts when we learn to wait on God.

Are you in a season of waiting right now? How can you find hope in this time? It can be difficult to stay, but it is in these moments that God shapes our character and deepens our trust. Reflect on how God has been faithful in past seasons of waiting and how He might be working in your heart now.

PRAYER

Lord, help me to trust you in the waiting. Teach me to find hope in your perfect timing, knowing that you are good and will fulfill Your promises. Strengthen my heart to wait quietly and patiently, confident that you are at work in my life. In Jesus' name, Amen.

LIVING WITH HOPE IN DIFFICULT TIMES

"In all this, you greatly rejoice, though now, for a little while, you may have had to suffer grief in all kinds of trials. These have come so that the proven genuineness of your faith—of greater worth than gold, which perishes even though refined by fire may result in praise, glory and honor when Jesus Christ is revealed."

Bible Verse: 1 Peter 1:6-7 (NIV)

Hope does not disappear in the midst of trials; it shines brightest in them. Peter encourages us to rejoice, even in suffering, because our trials test and refine our faith. Hope in difficult times doesn't mean ignoring pain but trusting that God will use our suffering for a greater purpose. Just as gold is refined by fire, our faith is purified through trials, and the result is something far more valuable. True hope does not look away from suffering but sees beyond it to the glory that is coming.

Are you facing difficult circumstances that feel overwhelming? How can you find hope in these moments? Consider that God is refining your faith and shaping you for something greater. Reflect on how you can choose hope in the midst of trials, knowing that they are preparing you for God's glory.

PRAYER

Father, I know that suffering is not without purpose in your plan. Help me to find hope in the midst of trials, trusting that you are refining my faith and preparing me for greater things. Strengthen me with the hope that in the end, all things will bring praise and glory to you. In Jesus' name, Amen.

HOPE FOR THE FUTURE

"For I know the plans I have for you," declares the Lord, "plans to prosper you and not to harm you, plans to give you hope and a future."

Bible Verse: Jeremiah 29:11 (NIV)

Hope is anchored in the assurance that God has a plan for our lives. This verse is a powerful reminder that God's plans for us are good, even when we cannot see the full picture. His plans are for our welfare, not for harm, and they lead us toward a future filled with hope. We can trust that God is always working for our good, even in moments of uncertainty or struggle. When we place our hope in His good plans, we can look toward the Future with confidence and peace.

Do you sometimes feel uncertain about the Future? How does this verse speak to your heart? God's plans are good, and

He will never lead you astray. Reflect on the areas of your life where you need to place more trust in His Future for you.

PRAYER

Lord, thank You for the hope You give me for the Future. I trust that Your plans for me are good, and I place my hope in Your ability to bring about good things, even when I don't understand what's happening now. Guide me as I walk into the Future You've prepared for me. In Jesus' name, Amen.

HOPE BEYOND THE PRESENT

"For in this hope, we were saved. But hope that is seen is no hope at all. Who hopes for what they already have? But if we hope for what we do not yet have, we wait for it patiently."

Bible Verse: Romans 8:24-25 (NIV)

Christian hope is unique because it reaches beyond the present reality into the eternal Future. The hope we have in Christ is not based on what we can see or experience now but is a confident expectation of what is to come. This hope sustains us through life's challenges, reminding us that the best is yet to come. While we wait for the fulfillment of God's promises, we hold on to the hope that we will experience eternal joy, peace, and restoration with Him. It is this hope of the Future that strengthens us to endure and persevere in the present.

What areas of your life are you hoping for change or restoration? How does knowing that God has promised you an eternal future filled with joy give you strength in the present? Reflect on how the hope of eternity can help you endure the challenges you face today.

PRAYER

Father, thank You for the eternal hope I have in Christ. Help me to fix my eyes on the future promise of joy and peace with You. Strengthen me to live with that hope, enduring patiently through the difficulties of this life, knowing that the best is yet to come. In Jesus' name, Amen.

LOVE

THE GREATEST COMMANDMENT: LOVE GOD

"Jesus replied: 'Love the Lord your God with all your heart and with all your soul and with all your mind.' This is the first and greatest commandment."

Bible Verse: Matthew 22:37-38 (NIV)

The greatest commandment is rooted in love—love for God above all else. This command calls us to love God with every part of our being: our heart (emotion), soul (identity), and mind (thoughts). Love for God isn't simply an abstract feeling but an all-encompassing devotion that shapes our actions, thoughts, and desires. Loving God with all that we are is the foundation for all other loves in our lives. When we fully commit ourselves to God's love, we open ourselves to experiencing His love in deeper and more transformative ways.

How can you love God more deeply today? Reflect on how your heart, soul, and mind can align to give God your best love. What areas of your life do you need to surrender more fully to Him? Loving God with our whole selves requires ongoing commitment and reflection.

PRAYER

Lord, I want to love you with all my heart, soul, and mind. Help me to grow in my love for you each day, allowing your love to guide my thoughts, actions, and decisions. Teach me how to love you more fully, and may my life reflect this love in everything I do. In Jesus' name, Amen.

LOVE YOUR NEIGHBOR

"And the second is like it: 'Love your neighbor as yourself.'"

Bible Verse: Matthew 22:39 (NIV)

Loving our neighbors is an extension of our love for God. Jesus emphasizes that the second greatest commandment is to love others in the same way we love ourselves. This means showing care, compassion, and kindness to those around us, regardless of their background, status, or differences. Love for others is not based on what they can offer us but on God's unconditional love for them. Loving others is a way we live out the love we have received from God, showing the world the depth and sincerity of our faith.

Who is your "neighbor"? Is there someone in your life who needs love and compassion today? How can you show love to those around you, especially those who may be difficult to love? Reflect on how God's love for you empowers you to love others unconditionally.

PRAYER

Father, thank You for showing me what true love looks like. Help me to love my neighbors as You love them—without conditions or limitations. Open my eyes to the needs of those around me, and give me the strength and wisdom to show Your love through my actions. In Jesus' name, Amen.

GOD'S LOVE FOR US

"This is how God showed his love among us: He sent his one and only Son into the world that we might live through him. This is love: not that we loved God, but that he loved us and sent his Son as an atoning sacrifice for our sins."

Bible Verse: 1 John 4:9-10 (NIV)

God's love for us is the ultimate example of sacrificial love. He didn't wait for us to come to Him or earn His love. Instead, He initiated love by sending His Son, Jesus, to die for our sins. This love is not based on our worth or goodness but is given freely and abundantly. God's love is sacrificial, unconditional, and selfless. It is a love that goes beyond emotions—it is an act of grace and mercy that brings us into a new life through Christ. Understanding and accepting God's love is the first step in experiencing true love.

How does the fact that God loved you first shape the way you view love? Reflect on the deepness of God's love, demonstrated by the sacrifice of His Son. How can you express your gratitude for such a love by loving others in return?

PRAYER

Thank You, Lord, for loving me with such a deep and sacrificial love. I am humbled by the gift of Your Son and the forgiveness you offer through Him. Help me to live in response to your love by loving others selflessly and generously. In Jesus' name, Amen.

THE NATURE OF TRUE LOVE

"Love is patient, love is kind. It does not envy, it does not boast, it is not proud. It does not dishonor others; it is not self-seeking; it is not easily angered; it keeps no record of wrongs. Love does not delight in evil but rejoices with the truth. It always protects, always trusts, always hopes, always perseveres."

Bible Verse: 1 Corinthians 13:4-7 (NIV)

True love, as described in 1 Corinthians 13, is selfless and sacrificial. It is not about what we can get from others but what we can give to them. It is patient and kind, never seeking its benefit but always seeking the good of others. True love isn't quick to anger or easily offended; it doesn't hold grudges. It always trusts and hopes, even in difficult circumstances. This kind of love reflects the heart of God and is the kind of love we are called to show others. It's not always easy, but it's always the right choice and reflects the love God has shown us.

Do you recognize this kind of love in your relationships? In what areas do you need to grow in love? Reflect on the qualities of love in this passage. Which qualities come most naturally to you, and which do you struggle with? How can you ask God to help you love others more like this?

PRAYER

Lord, help me to love others with the same love you have shown me—patiently, kindly, and selflessly. Teach me to embody the qualities of true love in my relationships. When love is difficult, remind me of your love for me, and help me to love with the same grace. In Jesus' name, Amen.

LOVE IN ACTION

"Dear children, let us not love with words or speech but with actions and in truth."

Bible Verse: 1 John 3:18 (NIV)

Love is not just something we say; it's something we do. Genuine love is demonstrated in actions, not just words. The Bible tells us that we must love "in truth" meaning our love should be sincere and not manipulative. Love is practical; it involves serving others, sacrificing for them, and caring for their needs. It's easy to say we love, but true love is seen in how we treat others, especially when it's inconvenient or challenging. Our love for others should reflect the love God has shown us, and it should be evident in what we do.

What actions can you take today to show love to someone in need? Reflect on the people in your life who may be longing for love practically. How can you be a reflection of God's love for them through your actions?

PRAYER

Lord, help me to love not just with my words but through my actions. Show me the needs around me and give me the heart to meet them. May my love be genuine and reflect your love in everything I do. In Jesus' name, Amen.

GRACE

THE MEANING OF GRACE

"For it is by grace you have been saved, through faith and this is not from yourselves, it is the gift of God not by works, so that no one can boast."

Bible Verse: Ephesians 2:8-9 (NIV)

Grace is God's unearned favor and kindness toward us. It is a gift that we can never earn through our efforts or good works. This verse emphasizes that salvation is by grace alone, through faith. We cannot boast about our goodness or achievements because our salvation is purely a result of God's generous grace. Grace means that God chooses to love us despite our flaws, mistakes, and shortcomings. It is not something we deserve but something God freely gives to us. Grace is foundational to our relationship with God and is what enables us to experience His love, mercy, and salvation.

How often do you reflect on the grace you've received from God? How does understanding that salvation is a gift, not a result of your efforts, change your perspective on your relationship with God? Take a moment to thank God for His undeserved grace and how it has transformed your life.

PRAYER

Heavenly Father, thank You for the gift of grace. I recognize that I could never earn your favor, yet you chose to give it to me freely. Help me to live in the light of your grace, and may I reflect your love and mercy to those around me. In Jesus' name, Amen.

GRACE IN OUR WEAKNESS

"But he said to me, 'My grace is sufficient for you, for my power is made perfect in weakness.' Therefore, I will boast all the more gladly of my weaknesses so that the power of Christ may rest upon me."

Bible Verse: 2 Corinthians 12:9 (NIV)

Grace is not only for salvation, but it also sustains us in our weakness. The Apostle Paul experienced personal struggles and weaknesses, and in response, God reminded him that His grace is sufficient. This means that God's grace doesn't just cover our sins but strengthens us in our frailties. In fact, God's power is most evident in our weakness because it shows that the strength we rely on is not our own but His. When we feel inadequate or incapable, God's grace enables us to keep moving forward, relying on His power and sufficiency rather than our strength.

Are you currently facing a weakness or struggle that feels overwhelming? How can you rely on God's grace to empower you in this moment? Reflect on how grace can transform your weaknesses into opportunities for God's power to shine.

PRAYER

Lord, thank You for Your sufficient grace. In my weaknesses, help me to rely on You fully, knowing that Your power is made perfect in my frailty. Please give me the strength to overcome my challenges, not by my power but by Yours. In Jesus' name, Amen.

GRACE IN FORGIVENESS

"Bear with each other and forgive one another if any of you has a grievance against someone. Forgive as the Lord forgave you."

Bible Verse: Colossians 3:13 (NIV)

Grace is the foundation of forgiveness. Just as God has forgiven us through the grace found in Christ, we are called to extend that same grace to others. Forgiveness is not always easy, especially when we feel hurt or wronged, but grace allows us to forgive as Christ has forgiven us. This doesn't mean forgetting or excusing the wrong, but it means choosing to release the offense and extend mercy. Grace in forgiveness brings healing and reconciliation, both with God and with others. It also sets us free from bitterness and resentment, allowing God's peace to fill our hearts.

Is there someone you are struggling to forgive? How does God's grace in your life empower you to forgive others? Reflect on the forgiveness you've received from God and how that grace can help you release others from their wrongs against you.

PRAYER

Father, thank You for the grace You have shown me in forgiving my sins. Please help me to extend that same grace to others, even when it is difficult. Give me the strength to forgive as You have forgiven me, and may Your grace bring healing to my heart and my relationships. In Jesus' name, Amen.

LIVING OUT GRACE

"For the grace of God has appeared that offers salvation to all people. It teaches us to say 'No' to ungodliness and worldly passions and to live self-controlled, upright and godly lives in this present age."

Bible Verse: Titus 2:11-12 (NIV)

God's grace is not just a passive gift, it is active and transformative. Grace teaches us how to live in response to God's love and salvation. It equips us to reject the temptation of sin and live a life that reflects God's goodness. Grace empowers us to live self-controlled, godly lives in the present age, regardless of the pressures or distractions around us. This grace is a constant teacher that guides our actions, attitudes, and decisions. Rather than being a license to live however we please, grace calls us to live with integrity and purpose, reflecting the holiness of God in our daily lives.

How does God's grace influence the way you live day by day? Are there areas in your life where you are struggling to live out the principles of grace? Reflect on the grace you've received and ask God to help you live in a way that honors Him.

PRAYER

Lord, thank You for Your transforming grace that teaches me to live a godly life. Help me to live with integrity and purpose, guided by Your grace in all that I do. Strengthen me to resist the temptations of this world and to reflect Your holiness in my actions. In Jesus' name, Amen.

GRACE FOR OTHERS

"Each of you should use whatever gift you have received to serve others as faithful stewards of God's grace in its various forms."

Bible Verse: 1 Peter 4:10 (NIV)

Grace is not something we should hoard for ourselves; it is a gift that is meant to be shared. God has given each of us unique gifts and abilities, and we are called to use them to serve others. In doing so, we become stewards of His grace, sharing it in its various forms. Whether through acts of kindness, service, encouragement, or teaching, we are called to extend grace to others. By using our gifts to serve, we reflect God's love and grace to a world in need. Grace is not just a gift to be received but a lifestyle to be lived out, blessing others and bringing glory to God.

How are you using your gifts to serve others? Are there ways you can be more intentional about showing grace to those around you? Reflect on the gifts God has given you and how you can use them to bless others with His grace.

PRAYER

Father, thank You for the grace You've extended to me. Help me to be a faithful steward of that grace, using the gifts You've given me to serve others. May my life be a reflection of Your love and mercy, blessing those around me with Your grace. In Jesus' name, Amen.

WISDOM

THE BEGINNING OF WISDOM

"The fear of the Lord is the beginning of wisdom, and knowledge of the Holy One is understanding."

Bible Verse: Proverbs 9:10 (NIV)

Wisdom begins with a proper reverence and awe for God. The "fear of the Lord" in this context is not about being afraid of God but recognizing His greatness, authority, and holiness. When we understand that God is the ultimate source of all wisdom, we begin to align our lives with His truth and purposes. Wisdom is not simply intellectual knowledge but involves a heart that is humble, teachable, and willing to follow God's guidance. True wisdom starts when we acknowledge that God is the foundation of all understanding and seek to live in accordance with His will.

How does your understanding of God influence the way you make decisions? Reflect on areas of your life where you need to humble yourself and seek God's wisdom. How can you start each day with a desire to honor God with your choices and actions?

PRAYER

Lord, I recognize that You are the source of all wisdom. Teach me to fear You, not in terror, but in awe and respect for Your greatness. Help me to seek Your wisdom above all else so that I may live in alignment with Your will. In Jesus' name, Amen.

WISDOM IN DECISION MAKING

"If any of you lacks wisdom, let him ask of God, who gives generously to all without finding fault, and it will be given to him."

Bible Verse: James 1:5 (NIV)

We all face decisions, big and small, in our lives. When we don't know what to do, God invites us to ask Him for wisdom. He promises to give wisdom generously to those who seek it without finding fault. Our understanding or mistakes do not limit God's wisdom; He gives it freely to those who approach Him with a sincere heart. Wisdom from God allows us to make choices that reflect His will and lead to peace. When we trust God's guidance, we can be confident that He will show us the path to take.

Are you facing a difficult decision? How can you ask God for wisdom in your situation? Reflect on the times when God has given you insight in the past and how it led you to make better decisions. Trust that He will guide you again when you seek Him.

PRAYER

Father, I ask for Your wisdom today. I trust that You will give it generously and without reproach. Guide me in my decisions and help me to choose the path that honors You. Give me clarity of mind and peace in knowing that You are leading me. In Jesus' name, Amen.

THE VALUE OF WISDOM

"Blessed are those who find wisdom, those who gain understanding, for *she is more profitable than silver and yields better returns than gold. She is more precious than rubies; nothing you desire can compare with her."*

Bible Verse: Proverbs 3:13-15 (NIV)

Wisdom is far more valuable than any material possession. It is described as being more precious than silver, gold, or rubies things we often think of as priceless. Yet wisdom offers returns that cannot be measured in financial terms. True wisdom brings peace, joy, and understanding, helping us navigate life's challenges with grace and clarity. It enriches our relationships, decision-making, and overall well-being. When we treasure wisdom above all else, we gain something far greater than wealth: a life that is aligned with God's purposes and filled with His blessings.

How do you value wisdom in your life? Are there areas where you have prioritized things of temporary value over lasting wisdom? Reflect on how you can seek wisdom in every area of your life and make it a priority, knowing that it will bring lasting rewards.

PRAYER

Lord, I recognize that wisdom is more valuable than anything this world can offer. Help me to seek wisdom above all else and to treasure it in my heart. Teach me to prioritize Your wisdom in my daily decisions and relationships. In Jesus' name, Amen.

TRUE WISDOM

"My goal is that they may be encouraged in heart and united in love, so that they may have the full riches of complete understanding, in order that they may know the mystery of God, namely, Christ, in whom are hidden all the treasures of wisdom and knowledge."

Bible Verse: Colossians 2:2-3 (NIV)

True wisdom is found in Christ. All the treasures of wisdom and knowledge are hidden in Him. To know Christ is to know the source of ultimate wisdom. Jesus is the embodiment of God's wisdom, and through Him, we have access to all that we need to live a godly life. Wisdom is not just an intellectual pursuit but a relational one. As we grow in our relationship with Jesus and seek to understand more about His character, teachings, and ways, we unlock the treasures of wisdom that will guide us in all areas of life.

How can a deeper relationship with Jesus help you grow in wisdom? Reflect on how seeking Christ more intimately leads to greater understanding and wisdom in your life. Spend time today learning more about His character and teachings.

PRAYER

Jesus, You are the source of all wisdom. I want to know You more deeply and experience the fullness of wisdom that is found in You. Help me to grow in my understanding of You and to live out the wisdom You offer. In Your name, Amen.

WISDOM IN OUR WORDS

"The tongue has the power of life and death, and those who love it will eat its fruit."

Bible Verse: Proverbs 18:21 (NIV)

Our words have power. They can build up or tear down, heal or hurt. Wisdom in speech comes from choosing our words carefully and thoughtfully. When we are wise in how we speak, we reflect God's heart, bringing life, encouragement, and truth to those around us. The Bible warns that the tongue can bring destruction if not controlled, but with wisdom, it can be used to bless and give life. Wisdom, in our words, means speaking truth in love, offering encouragement, and refraining from gossip or hurtful speech.

How do your words reflect the wisdom of God? Are there areas where you need to be more thoughtful or kind in your speech? Reflect on the power of your words and how you can use them to build others up and bring life.

PRAYER

Lord, help me to be wise in my speech. Guard my heart and mind so that my words may reflect Your love and truth. Give me the wisdom to speak life into the people around me and to use my words to bring honor to You. In Jesus' name, Amen.

DISCERNMENT

SEEKING GOD FOR DISCERNMENT

"If any of you lacks wisdom, let him ask of God, who gives generously to all without finding fault, and it will be given to him."

Bible Verse: James 1:5 (NIV)

Discernment begins with seeking God. The Bible encourages us to ask God for wisdom and discernment, and He promises to give it generously. Discernment is the ability to judge rightly and make wise decisions, especially in situations where the right choice is not obvious. God's wisdom equips us to see things from His perspective, understanding what is right, good, and true. Discernment isn't something we can develop on our own but something that comes from God through His Holy Spirit.

When we seek God's guidance with a humble heart, He provides the discernment we need.

Are you currently facing a situation where you need discernment? Take a moment to ask God for His wisdom in making the right decision. Reflect on times when God has given you clarity and guidance in the past, and trust that He will do it again.

PRAYER

Father, I ask for your discernment in the decisions I am facing. Help me to see things clearly and make choices that align with your will. Give me the wisdom to understand your guidance and follow it wholeheartedly. In Jesus' name, Amen.

DISCERNMENT IN TESTING

"Dear friends, do not believe every spirit, but test the spirits to see whether they are from God because many false prophets have gone out into the world."

Bible Verse: 1 John 4:1 (NIV)

Discernment is essential in distinguishing between what is true and what is false. In a world filled with competing voices and ideas, we are called to test what we hear against the truth of God's Word. Not every idea or teaching is from God, and discernment helps us to recognize what aligns with God's truth. This involves testing the spirit behind the message—not just the message itself. We need to be sensitive to the leading of the Holy Spirit, who guides us into all truth. Discernment allows us to protect ourselves from deception and live in alignment with God's will.

What voices or teachings are influencing your decisions and beliefs? How can you test them against God's truth? Reflect on how you can be more discerning in the information you consume and the people you listen to. Ask the Holy Spirit to guide you in truth.

PRAYER

Lord, help me to be discerning in all that I hear and see. Guard my heart and mind against false teachings, and help me to test everything by Your Word. Teach me to listen to your voice and follow your truth above all else. In Jesus' name, Amen.

THE ROLE OF THE HOLY SPIRIT IN DISCERNMENT

"But when he, the spirit of truth, comes, he will guide you into all the truth. He will not speak on his own; he will speak only what he hears, and he will tell you what is yet to come."

Bible Verse: John 16:13 (NIV)

The Holy Spirit plays a central role in providing discernment. As the "Spirit of truth," He guides us into all truth and helps us understand God's will in any situation. Discernment isn't just about having good judgment—it is about being attuned to the Holy Spirit's leading. The spirit reveals God's heart to us, bringing clarity when we face decisions, challenges, or uncertainty. When we walk in step with the Holy Spirit, He empowers us to discern what is true, right, and best, even when the choices are difficult or unclear.

How sensitive are you to the Holy Spirit's guidance in your life? Reflect on times when the Holy Spirit has guided you or given you discernment in a decision. How can you cultivate a deeper sensitivity to His voice and leading?

PRAYER

Holy Spirit, thank You for guiding me into all truth. I ask that you open my ears and heart to your leading. Help me to follow you closely and trust your discernment in every decision I face. Speak to me clearly and give me the courage to obey. In Jesus' name, Amen.

DISCERNMENT IN RELATIONSHIPS

"The righteous choose their friends carefully, but the way of the wicked leads them astray."

Bible Verse: Proverbs 12:26 (NIV)

Discernment is crucial when it comes to relationships. The people we surround ourselves with influence our thoughts, actions, and even our spiritual walk. The Bible encourages us to choose our friends wisely and to be discerning in our relationships. Discernment helps us recognize who is a positive influence and who may be leading us away from God. This doesn't mean we avoid everyone who doesn't share our faith, but it does mean being intentional about the depth and nature of our relationships. Wise discernment in relationships protects us from harmful influences and helps us build connections that encourage us in our faith.

Are there relationships in your life where you need discernment? How do the people around you influence your thoughts and actions? Reflect on how God might be leading you to strengthen or redefine certain relationships in your life for your spiritual growth.

PRAYER

Father, give me discernment in my relationships. Help me to choose friends and companions who will encourage me in my faith and draw me closer to You. Show me if any relationships are leading me astray, and help me to make wise choices. In Jesus' name, Amen.

LIVING WITH DISCERNMENT IN THE WORLD

"And this is my prayer: that your love may abound more and more in knowledge and depth of insight so that you may be able to discern what is best and may be pure and blameless for the day of Christ."

Bible Verse: Philippians 1:9-10 (NIV)

As Christians, we are called to live with discernment in a world that often promotes values that are contrary to God's will. Discernment helps us to navigate this world with wisdom, making choices that reflect our love for God and others. The Apostle Paul prays that believers would grow in knowledge and insight so they can discern what is best, not just what is acceptable. Discernment in the Christian life involves a continual process of growing in our understanding of God's Word and applying it to our daily lives. It enables us to live pure and blameless lives in anticipation of Christ's return.

Are there areas of your life where you need to grow in discernment to reflect God's best? Reflect on how God's wisdom can help you navigate the challenges of living in this world while staying true to your faith. How can you continue to grow in your love for God through increased discernment?

PRAYER

Lord, I pray that my love for you would abound more and more and that you would give me the wisdom and insight to discern what is best. Help me to live a life that is pure and blameless, reflecting your truth in all I do. Continue to grow me in discernment as I seek to honor you. In Jesus' name, Amen.

RENEWAL

THE NEED FOR RENEWAL

"Do not conform to the pattern of this world, but be transformed by the renewing of your mind. Then you will be able to test and approve what God's will is—his good, pleasing and perfect will."

Bible Verse: Romans 12:2 (NIV)

Renewal begins in the mind. The world constantly tries to shape us, molding our thoughts, values, and priorities to fit its standards. But as believers, we are called to be different—to be transformed by the renewing of our minds. This renewal happens when we allow God's Word and the Holy Spirit to reshape our thinking. When our minds are renewed, we can discern God's will for our lives and live in a way that reflects His goodness. Renewal is not a one-time event but a continual process that happens as we stay close to God and remain in His Word.

Are there areas in your life where the patterns of the world have influenced your thinking? How can you begin the process of renewal in your mind? Reflect on the importance of God's Word and His Spirit in renewing your thoughts and attitudes.

PRAYER

Lord, I ask for a renewal of my mind. Help me not to be shaped by the world but to be transformed by Your Word. Guide my thoughts so that I may know and follow Your will for my life. Renew me each day through Your presence and truth. In Jesus' name, Amen.

SPIRITUAL RENEWAL THROUGH GOD'S WORD

"I am laid low in the dust; preserve my life according to your word."

Bible Verse: Psalm 119:25 (NIV)

God's word is powerful and life-giving. When we feel spiritually worn out or weighed down by life's struggles, it is God's Word that can revive and renew us. The psalmist expresses a deep reliance on God's Word for life and renewal. Just as food nourishes the body, the Word of God nourishes the soul, giving us strength, encouragement, and direction. Renewal happens when we immerse ourselves in Scripture, allowing it to speak life into our dry, weary hearts. The more we read, meditate, and apply God's Word, the more we experience spiritual renewal.

When was the last time God's Word brought renewal to your heart? Reflect on how Scripture has been a source of strength during tough times. How can you prioritize spending time in God's Word to experience the renewal it offers?

PRAYER

Father, Your Word is a source of life and renewal. When I feel weary, help me to turn to Your Word for strength and encouragement. Open my eyes to the truths that will refresh and restore me. May Your Word continually renew my spirit. In Jesus' name, Amen.

RENEWAL IN THE SPIRIT

"He saved us, not because of righteous things we had done, but because of his mercy. He saved us through the washing of rebirth and renewal by the Holy Spirit."

Bible Verse: Titus 3:5 (NIV)

Renewal comes through the Holy Spirit. When we come to faith in Christ, we experience a spiritual rebirth, and the Holy Spirit begins the work of renewal in our hearts. This renewal isn't about improving ourselves by our efforts but about God's mercy and the transforming power of the Holy Spirit. He cleanses us, making us new and empowering us to live according to God's will. Spiritual renewal is an ongoing process as the Holy Spirit works in our lives, drawing us closer to God, convicting us of sin, and transforming our hearts and minds.

Have you experienced the renewal of the Holy Spirit in your life? How can you cooperate with the spirit's work of transformation in you? Reflect on areas where you need the Holy Spirit to bring renewal and ask Him to continue His work in your heart.

PRAYER

Holy Spirit, thank You for the work of renewal in my life. I invite You to continue transforming me, making me more like Christ. Cleanse my heart, renew my spirit, and empower me to live for God's glory. Help me to stay in step with You and trust in Your transformative power. In Jesus' name, Amen.

RENEWED STRENGTH IN THE LORD

"But those who hope in the Lord will renew their strength. They will soar on wings like eagles; they will run and not grow weary; they will walk and not be faint."

Bible Verse: Isaiah 40:31 (NIV)

Renewal brings strength—strength that comes from God alone. When we place our hope in the Lord, He renews our strength, enabling us to face life's challenges with endurance and confidence. This promise from Isaiah reminds us that God gives us strength to persevere. Like eagles soaring high, we can rise above our struggles and difficulties when we rely on God's power. Renewal in the Lord allows us to keep moving forward without growing weary, trusting that He will sustain us through every season of life.

Are you feeling physically or spiritually exhausted? Reflect on where your strength is coming from. How can you lean into God for renewed strength in your current situation? Take a moment to rest in God's promises and trust that He will renew your energy and spirit.

PRAYER

Lord, I place my hope in You today. Thank You for the promise of renewed strength. Help me to rest in Your power and to rely on You when I feel weak. Lift me when I grow weary and empower me to run the race You've set before me. In Jesus' name, Amen.

THE RENEWAL OF OUR HEARTS

"Therefore, we do not lose heart. Though outwardly we are wasting away, yet inwardly we are being renewed day by day."

Bible Verse: 2 Corinthians 4:16 (NIV)

The renewal we experience in Christ is not just external, but it touches the deepest parts of our being—our hearts. Life can take a toll on us, and we may feel worn out or discouraged. But in Christ, we are being renewed inwardly, day by day. This renewal doesn't happen all at once; it's a continuous process of being shaped by God's love, grace, and truth. Even in the midst of trials, God is at work in our hearts, making us more like Christ. This daily renewal strengthens us to face life's challenges with hope and perseverance.

Are there areas in your heart where you feel weary or burdened? Reflect on the promise that God is renewing you inwardly, no matter what you face outwardly. How can you embrace the daily renewal God offers through His presence in your life?

PRAYER

Father, I thank you for the promise of renewal, both inside and out. Even when I feel discouraged or tired, I trust that you are renewing my heart day by day. Help me to embrace your work of transformation in my life and to rely on Your strength. In Jesus' name, Amen.

TRANSFORMATION

THE POWER OF GOD'S TRANSFORMING GRACE

"Therefore, if anyone is in Christ, the new creation has come: The old has gone, the new is here!"

Bible Verse: 2 Corinthians 5:17 (NIV)

Transformation in Christ begins with a radical change in who we are. When we come to faith in Jesus, we are not just improved or slightly altered; we are made completely new. Our old life, marked by sin and separation from God, is gone, and a new life in Christ begins. This transformation is the work of God's grace, which empowers us to live differently—living in a way that reflects Christ's love and holiness. Transformation is not about doing better; it's about being made new by God's power. We become a new creation, equipped to live out God's purposes for our lives.

Have you fully embraced your new identity in Christ? Reflect on the changes God has made in your life since you came to faith in Him. How can you walk in the fullness of this transformation each day?

PRAYER

Lord, thank You for making me a new creation in Christ. Help me to embrace this transformation daily and live according to the new life You've given me. May my life reflect Your love and holiness as I walk in the newness of life. In Jesus' name, Amen.

TRANSFORMATION BY THE RENEWING OF THE MIND

"Do not conform to the pattern of this world, but be transformed by the renewing of your mind. Then you will be able to test and approve what God's will is—his good, pleasing and perfect will."

Bible Verse: Romans 12:2 (NIV)

Transformation begins in the mind. The world around us constantly tries to shape our thoughts, values, and priorities. But as believers, we are called to be transformed by the renewing of our minds. This happens when we choose to align our thinking with God's truth, allowing His Word to reshape our views and desires. Transformation of the mind enables us to discern God's will and live in ways that honor Him. It's an ongoing process as we continually allow God's truth to challenge and change the way we think.

Are there areas of your thinking that need to be renewed? Reflect on how the truth of God's Word can transform your mind and align it more closely with His will. How can you make space for His truth to reshape your thoughts and attitudes?

PRAYER

Father, I ask for the transformation of my mind. Help me not to conform to the patterns of this world but to be renewed by Your Word. Teach me to think in ways that reflect Your will and bring honor to You. In Jesus' name, Amen.

THE HOLY SPIRIT'S ROLE IN TRANSFORMATION

"But we ought always to thank God for you, brothers and sisters, loved by the Lord because God chose you as first fruits to be saved through the sanctifying work of the Spirit and belief in the truth."

Bible Verse: 2 Thessalonians 2:13 (NIV)

The Holy Spirit plays a central role in the process of transformation. When we come to Christ, we are saved through the sanctifying work of the Holy Spirit, who is the agent of our ongoing transformation. Sanctification means being set apart and made holy, and this process is a work of the spirit in our lives. Through the Holy Spirit, we are empowered to live according to God's will and grow in holiness. The transformation the spirit brings isn't just external—it's internal, changing our hearts, desires, and attitudes to reflect the character of Christ.

How have you experienced the Holy Spirit's transformative work in your life? Reflect on the areas where the spirit is leading you to grow and change. How can you cooperate more fully with the spirit's work of transformation in your heart?

PRAYER

Holy Spirit, thank You for Your work of transformation in my life. I invite You to continue to sanctify me and make me more like Christ. Help me to listen to Your guidance and cooperate with the work You are doing in my heart. In Jesus' name, Amen.

TRANSFORMATION THROUGH SURRENDER

"I have been crucified with Christ, and I no longer live, but Christ lives in me. The life I now live in the body, I live by faith in the Son of God, who loved me and gave himself for me."

Bible Verse: Galatians 2:20 (NIV)

Transformation requires surrender—surrender of our old self and our desires to Christ. The Apostle Paul speaks of being crucified with Christ, meaning that his old life, shaped by sin and selfishness, has been put to death. In its place, Christ now lives in him. This is the essence of transformation: it's not about us living for ourselves but allowing Christ to live in and through us. True transformation happens when we surrender control to Jesus and let His life be manifested in ours. It's a continual process of laying down our desires and embracing the life Christ has for us.

Is there an area of your life where you are struggling to surrender to Christ? Reflect on what it means to be crucified with Christ and how this surrender leads to true transformation. How can you fully allow Christ to live in and through you?

PRAYER

Jesus, I surrender my life to you. Help me to lay down my desires and embrace the life you have for me. May Your Spirit live in me and transform me daily so that I may reflect your love and truth to the world. In Jesus' name, Amen.

THE FRUIT OF TRANSFORMATION

"But the fruit of the spirit is love, joy, peace, forbearance, kindness, goodness, faithfulness, gentleness and self-control. Against such things, there is no law."

Bible Verse: Galatians 5:22-23 (NIV)

Transformation is not just about inner change; it's about the outward evidence of that change in our lives. The fruit of the spirit is the tangible result of the Holy Spirit's transformative work in us. As God's Spirit transforms us, we begin to bear fruit that reflects His character. Love, joy, peace, kindness, and all the other fruits listed in this passage become evident in our lives. Transformation leads to a life that reflects Christ's character in every way, and as we grow in the spirit, these fruits become more and more visible in our daily actions and attitudes.

Which of the fruits of the spirit are most evident in your life? Which do you feel you need more of? Reflect on how the transformation the Holy Spirit is bringing to your life should show up in your relationships, actions, and attitudes. How can you cultivate more of this fruit?

PRAYER

Lord, thank You for the fruit of the Spirit that You are growing in me. Help me bear more of these fruits in my life and reflect Your character in all I do. May Your transformative work in me be evident to those around me, bringing glory to Your name. In Jesus' name, Amen.

SPIRITUAL DISCIPLINE

THE IMPORTANCE OF SPIRITUAL DISCIPLINE

"Have nothing to do with godless myths and old wives' tales; rather, train yourself to be godly. For physical training is of some value, but godliness has value for all things, holding promise for both the present life and the life to come."

Bible Verse: 1 Timothy 4:7-8 (NIV)

Spiritual discipline is essential for growing in godliness and strengthening our relationship with God. Just as physical training helps us develop strength and endurance, spiritual discipline helps us develop spiritual strength. It's an intentional, ongoing practice that shapes us into the image of Christ. The Bible teaches that while physical exercise has its benefits, spiritual discipline has even greater value—lasting value that impacts not only this life but the life to come. Disciplines such as prayer, Bible study, fasting, and worship train us to live in alignment with God's will and grow in our faith.

Are there areas of your spiritual life that you need to give more attention to? Reflect on the importance of training yourself to be godly and how consistent spiritual practices can shape your heart and mind. How can you incorporate more spiritual discipline into your routine?

PRAYER

Lord, help me to commit to spiritual discipline in my life. Teach me to train myself in godliness so that I may grow closer to You. Give me the strength to stay faithful to the practices that nurture my relationship with You. In Jesus' name, Amen.

DISCIPLINE THROUGH PRAYER

"But Jesus often withdrew to lonely places and prayed."

Bible Verse: Luke 5:16 (NIV)

Jesus set the perfect example for us when it comes to the discipline of prayer. Despite His busy ministry, He made time to pray—often withdrawing to quiet places to spend time with His Father. Prayer is not just a way to ask God for things but a discipline that keeps us connected to Him, deepening our relationship and dependence on Him. Through prayer, we align our hearts with God's will, express our gratitude, seek His guidance, and grow in trust. Spiritual discipline involves making prayer a regular, intentional part of our lives, just as Jesus did.

How often do you set aside time for prayer? Reflect on the importance of making prayer a discipline in your life. How can you create a routine for prayer, just as Jesus did, to deepen your connection with God?

PRAYER

Father, teach me to prioritize prayer in my life. Help me to follow Jesus' example and withdraw from the busyness of life to spend time with you. May my heart grow closer to you as I cultivate this discipline of prayer. In Jesus' name, Amen.

DISCIPLINE THROUGH THE WORD OF GOD

"All Scripture is God-breathed and is useful for teaching, rebuking, correcting and training in righteousness, so that the servant of God may be thoroughly equipped for every good work."

Bible Verse: 2 Timothy 3:16-17 (NIV)

The Bible is the primary tool God uses to equip us for a life of godliness. Reading, meditating on, and studying Scripture are essential spiritual disciplines that help us grow in knowledge and righteousness. God's word teaches us what is right, corrects our mistakes, and trains us in how to live a life that honors Him. Spiritual discipline involves making time to engage with the Bible regularly, allowing its truths to shape our thoughts, attitudes, and actions. The more we invest in

Scripture, the better equipped we are to live out God's calling for our lives.

How consistent are you in reading and studying the Bible? Reflect on how God's Word has impacted your life and how it continues to shape you. What steps can you take to develop a deeper habit of reading Scripture and applying it to your life?

PRAYER

Lord, thank You for Your Word, which teaches, corrects, and equips me for every good work. Help me to make Scripture a daily discipline in my life. Open my heart to Your truths, and guide me to live according to Your Word. In Jesus' name, Amen.

FASTING AS A SPIRITUAL DISCIPLINE

"When you fast, do not look somber as the hypocrites do, for they disfigure their faces to show others they are fasting. Truly, I tell you, they have received their reward in full. But when you fast, anoint your head and wash your face, so that it will not be obvious to others that you are fasting, but only to your unseen Father; and your Father, who sees what is done in secret, will reward you."

Bible Verse: Matthew 6:16-18 (NIV)

Fasting is a powerful spiritual discipline that helps us focus on God, humble ourselves, and grow in dependence on Him. Jesus doesn't say "if you fast" but "when you fast," indicating that fasting is a practice that should be a part of our spiritual lives. It's not about drawing attention to ourselves or showing off our sacrifices but about seeking God more deeply. Fasting reminds us that God is our true sustenance, and it creates space in our hearts for Him to work. When done with the right heart, fasting leads to spiritual breakthroughs, increased sensitivity to God, and a more profound connection with Him.

Have you ever fasted? Reflect on the role fasting could play in your spiritual life. How can you incorporate fasting as a discipline to deepen your dependence on God and grow spiritually?

PRAYER

Lord, teach me the discipline of fasting so that I may grow closer to You. Help me to fast with the right heart—not for the approval of others but for a deeper connection with You. May this discipline draw me closer to Your will and strengthen my faith. In Jesus' name, Amen.

DISCIPLINE THROUGH OBEDIENCE

"Jesus replied, 'Anyone who loves me will obey my teaching. My Father will love them, and we will come to them and make our home with them.'"

Bible Verse: John 14:23 (NIV)

Spiritual discipline isn't just about what we do; it's about how we live in response to God's love and commands. Jesus makes it clear that obedience is a vital part of our relationship with Him. Obeying His commands is not a burden but an expression of love for Him. When we make obedience a discipline in our lives, we invite God to make His home in us, and we experience greater intimacy with Him. Discipline through obedience requires us to trust God's wisdom, even when it's hard, and to choose to follow His guidance daily.

How does your obedience to God reflect your love for Him? Reflect on areas of your life where you may struggle with obedience. How can you strengthen this discipline of following God's commands and walking in His will?

PRAYER

Lord, help me to obey You out of love and gratitude for all that You've done for me. Teach me to follow Your commands faithfully, knowing that obedience brings me closer to You. Help me to trust Your wisdom in all things and live in a way that honors You. In Jesus' name, Amen.

SELF-CONTROL

THE FOUNDATION OF SELF-CONTROL

"But the fruit of the spirit is love, joy, peace, forbearance, kindness, goodness, faithfulness, gentleness and self-control. Against such things, there is no law."

Bible Verse: Galatians 5:22-23 (NIV)

Self-control is a fruit of the spirit, meaning it is something that God produces in us as we walk in the spirit. It is not simply about willpower or restraint but about being yielded to God's guidance and allowing the Holy Spirit to empower us to make wise, disciplined choices. Self-control involves the ability to manage our impulses, emotions, and desires in a way that honors God. As we grow in the fruit of the spirit, we begin to exhibit self-control in every area of our lives—from our speech to our actions, thoughts, and even our attitudes.

Where do you struggle most with self-control? Reflect on areas of your life where you might be giving in to impulses or desires that don't honor God. How can you rely more on the Holy Spirit to develop greater self-control in your life?

PRAYER

Father, thank You for giving me the Holy Spirit to help me develop self-control. Empower me to resist temptations and make choices that honor You. Help me to cultivate the fruit of self-control so that my life reflects Your love and righteousness. In Jesus' name, Amen.

SELF-CONTROL IN THE FACE OF TEMPTATION

"No temptation has overtaken you except what is common to humanity. And God is faithful; he will not let you be tempted beyond what you can bear. But when you are tempted, he will also provide a way out so that you can endure it."

Bible Verse: 1 Corinthians 10:13 (NIV)

Temptation is a reality for all of us, but God's Word assures us that we are never without a way out. Self-control in the face of temptation involves recognizing the escape routes God provides and choosing to take them. This requires vigilance, humility, and an active reliance on God's strength to resist. Self-control isn't about avoiding temptation altogether but about handling it with wisdom and strength from God when it comes. God's faithfulness ensures that no temptation is too great for us to bear, and He equips us with the tools we need to endure.

Think about the temptations you face regularly. How do you handle them? Reflect on the promise that God provides a way out and the importance of recognizing and choosing that way. How can you strengthen your resolve and rely on God in those moments?

PRAYER

Lord, I thank You for Your faithfulness in providing a way out when I am tempted. Help me to recognize the escape routes You provide and give me the strength to choose them. Teach me to rely on Your power, not my own, when facing temptation. In Jesus' name, Amen.

SELF-CONTROL IN OUR WORDS

"*A gentle* answer *turns away wrath, but a harsh word stirs up anger.*"

Bible Verse: Proverbs 15:1 (NIV)

Our words are powerful, and practicing self-control in our speech is essential for living a life that reflects God's love. Self-control, in our words, means choosing to speak with kindness, gentleness, and wisdom, even when emotions run high. A gentle answer can diffuse conflict and prevent misunderstandings, while harsh words only escalate tension. The ability to control our tongues is a sign of maturity and wisdom, and it requires constant self-discipline. By allowing the Holy Spirit to guide our speech, we can build others up rather than tearing them down.

How do you typically respond when someone angers or frustrates you? Reflect on the impact of your words and how self-control can help you respond with grace, even in difficult situations. How can you cultivate more control over your speech in everyday conversations?

PRAYER

Father, help me to exercise self-control in my speech. Guard my heart and mind so that I may respond with kindness and wisdom, especially in moments of tension. May my words reflect your love and bring peace to those around me. In Jesus' name, Amen.

SELF-CONTROL IN DESIRES AND ACTIONS

"For the grace of God has appeared that offers salvation to all people. It teaches us to say 'No' to ungodliness and worldly passions and to live self-controlled, upright and godly lives in this present age."

Bible Verse: Titus 2:11-12 (NIV)

Self-control is essential for living a godly life in a world full of distractions and temptations. This verse reminds us that God's grace not only saves us but also teaches us to live in a way that honors Him. It enables us to say "no" to ungodliness and worldly desires that pull us away from God's will. True self-control is not about suppressing our desires but about aligning our desires with God's purposes for our lives. It's about choosing what pleases God over what pleases the flesh. Living self-controlled lives requires us to be intentional and disciplined in our thoughts, actions, and decisions.

What desires or passions in your life need to be surrendered to God? Reflect on how God's grace empowers you to say no to things that pull you away from His will. How can you cultivate a deeper sense of self-control in the way you live and make decisions?

PRAYER

Lord, thank You for the grace that teaches me to live self-controlled, godly lives. Help me to say no to ungodliness and worldly passions and to say yes to the things that honor You. Empower me to live in a way that reflects Your goodness in every area of my life. In Jesus' name, Amen.

THE REWARD OF SELF-CONTROL

"Do you not know that in a race, all the runners run, but only one gets the prize? Run in such a way as to get the prize. Everyone who competes in the games goes into strict training. They do it to get a crown that will not last, but we do it to get a crown that will last forever."

Bible Verse: 1 Corinthians 9:24-25 (NIV)

Self-control is not always easy, but it brings lasting rewards. Paul compares the Christian life to an athlete training for a race. Just as athletes train with discipline to win a temporary prize, we are called to practice self-control for an eternal reward. The rewards of self-control in our lives go beyond temporary satisfaction; they lead to spiritual growth, a deeper relationship with God, and infinite blessings. Just as athletes deny themselves certain comforts to train for a prize, we are called to deny worldly desires to pursue the eternal rewards God has for us.

What rewards are you running after in your life? Reflect on how practicing self-control leads to greater rewards, not just in this life but for eternity. How can you stay focused on the eternal prize, even when temptations seem appealing?

PRAYER

Father, help me to run the race of life with self-control and endurance. Remind me that the rewards of this world are fleeting, but the crown You offer lasts forever. Give me the strength to discipline myself in ways that honor You and lead to eternal rewards. In Jesus' name, Amen.

PEACE

THE SOURCE OF TRUE PEACE

"Peace I leave with you; my peace I give you. I do not give to you as the world gives. Do not let your hearts be troubled, and do not be afraid."

Bible Verse: John 14:27 (NIV)

True peace is a gift from Jesus, and it's different from the peace that the world offers. The world's peace is often circumstantial, dependent on external factors such as our relationships, success, or comfort. But the peace Jesus offers transcends circumstances. It is a deep, abiding peace that remains even in the midst of trials. When we receive Jesus' peace, we can have calm in our hearts, even when the world around us is chaotic. This peace is rooted in trusting Him, knowing that He is in control and that His presence gives us the strength to endure.

Do you find yourself searching for peace in external circumstances, or are you seeking peace in Jesus? Reflect on how you can more fully trust in His peace, especially in times of uncertainty or difficulty.

PRAYER

Jesus, thank You for the peace You offer me. Help me to rest in Your peace, no matter what is happening around me. May my heart be free from fear and anxiety, trusting in Your presence and sovereignty. In Your name, Amen.

PEACE IN THE MIDST OF TRIALS

"Do not be anxious about anything, but in every situation, by prayer and petition, with thanksgiving, present your requests to God. And the peace of God, which transcends all understanding, will guard your hearts and your minds in Christ Jesus."

Bible Verse: Philippians 4:6-7 (NIV)

Peace doesn't mean the absence of problems; it means trusting God in the middle of them. Paul encourages us not to be anxious but to bring everything to God in prayer. As we present our concerns to God, His peace, which surpasses human understanding, will guard our hearts and minds. This peace isn't based on a lack of problems but on the confidence that God is in control and He is working in every situation for our good. True peace comes when we surrender our worries to God and allow His peace to guard our hearts.

What anxieties are you holding onto today? Reflect on how you can surrender them to God in prayer. How can God's peace guard your heart and mind in the midst of your current challenges?

PRAYER

Lord, I bring my anxieties before You today. Help me to release them into Your hands and trust that You are in control. Fill my heart with Your peace, and guard my mind from worry and fear. Thank You for Your peace that surpasses all understanding. In Jesus' name, Amen.

PEACE WITH GOD

"Therefore, since we have been justified through faith, we have peace with God through our Lord Jesus Christ."

Bible Verse: Romans 5:1 (NIV)

Peace begins with being reconciled to God. Before we know Christ, we are at enmity with God because of our sins. But through faith in Jesus, we are justified—declared righteous—and made right with God. This reconciliation brings us peace with God. It's a peace that removes the barrier of sin and brings us into a relationship with the Creator of the universe. This peace doesn't depend on our performance but on Jesus' finished work on the cross. Because of Jesus, we can now approach God without fear, knowing that we have peace with Him.

Have you fully embraced the peace that comes from being reconciled with God through Jesus? Reflect on how the peace of being in right standing with God changes the way you live and approach Him.

PRAYER

Father, thank You for the peace I have with You through Jesus Christ. I am grateful for the reconciliation that His death and resurrection have provided. Help me to live in the fullness of this peace, and may my relationship with You be one of trust and joy. In Jesus' name, Amen.

PEACE WITH OTHERS

"If it is possible, as far as it depends on you, live at peace with everyone."

Bible Verse: Romans 12:18 (NIV)

Peace is not only about our relationship with God; it also extends to our relationships with others. Living at peace with everyone can be difficult, especially when conflicts arise. However, the Bible encourages us to do everything in our power to maintain peace. We may not always be able to control others' responses, but we can control our actions and attitudes. Being a peacemaker means showing kindness, forgiveness, and humility, even when it's hard. It's actively seeking peace and reconciliation, not division and strife.

Are there relationships in your life where peace needs to be restored? Reflect on how you can be a peacemaker, actively pursuing peace through forgiveness, understanding, and love. How can you take the first step toward reconciliation today?

PRAYER

Lord, help me to live at peace with those around me. Give me the humility and wisdom to seek reconciliation and to be a peacemaker. When conflict arises, may I respond with love and patience, seeking Your peace in all relationships? In Jesus' name, Amen.

THE PEACE THAT GUARDS OUR HEARTS

"Let the peace of Christ rule in your hearts, since as members of one body you were called to peace. And be thankful."

Bible Verse: Colossians 3:15 (NIV)

Peace in Christ is meant to rule our hearts. The word "rule" in this verse means to act as an umpire or guide. The peace of Christ should be the deciding factor in our emotions, decisions, and actions. When Christ's peace reigns in our hearts, it calms our anxieties, brings clarity in decision-making, and guides us toward unity with others. As members of the body of Christ, we are called to live in peace, and this peace is not just an emotion but a lifestyle—a deep, abiding trust in God's sovereignty and goodness.

Does Christ's peace rule in your heart, or do anxiety and unrest often take control? Reflect on how the peace of Christ can act as an umpire in your decisions and relationships. How can you intentionally allow His peace to guide your thoughts and actions?

PRAYER

Jesus, I invite your peace to rule in my heart. Help me to trust in your sovereignty and allow your peace to guide my decisions, thoughts, and relationships. May your peace be a testimony of your presence in my life. In Jesus' name, Amen.

JOY

JOY IN TRIALS

"Consider it pure joy, my brothers and sisters, whenever you face trials of many kinds because you know that the testing of your faith produces perseverance."

Bible Verse: James 1:2-3 (NIV)

Joy is often misunderstood as being dependent on favorable circumstances, but the Bible teaches that joy can coexist with hardship. James challenges us to consider it "pure joy" when we face trials because these moments test our faith and build perseverance. It is not that we should be happy about the suffering itself, but rather, we can rejoice knowing that God uses our trials to refine and strengthen us. True joy is found in the understanding that God is at work in all situations, even the difficult ones and that our faith will grow as we trust Him through them.

When you face difficulties, how do you respond? Reflect on how viewing trials as opportunities for growth can change your perspective. How can you choose joy, knowing that God is using your struggles for your good and His glory?

PRAYER

Lord, help me to find joy even in the midst of trials. Strengthen my faith through every challenge and help me to trust that you are refining me for something greater. May your joy fill my heart as I persevere in Your name. Amen.

JOY IN OBEDIENCE

"If you keep my commands, you will remain in my love, just as I have kept my Father's commands and remain in his love. I have told you this so that my joy may be in you and that your joy may be complete."

Bible Verse: John 15:10-11 (NIV)

Obedience to God is often seen as a duty or obligation, but Jesus tells us that it is also the pathway to joy. When we obey God, we remain in His love and experience the fullness of joy that comes from living in accordance with His will. Jesus' joy becomes our joy when we align our lives with His commands, not out of fear or legalism, but out of love and trust in His goodness. This joy is not temporary or circumstantial—it is deep, fulfilling, and complete, knowing that we are living in harmony with the Creator.

How does obedience to God bring joy into your life? Reflect on the areas where you may struggle with obedience and consider how following God's will can lead to deeper joy. How can you choose joy in your relationship with God through obedience?

PRAYER

Jesus, thank You for showing me that true joy comes through obedience to your commands. Help me to obey not out of obligation but out of love for you. Fill me with your joy as I follow your will and experience the peace that comes with living in harmony with You. Amen.

JOY IN SERVING OTHERS

"In everything I did, I showed you that by this kind of hard work, we must help the weak, remembering the words the Lord Jesus himself said: 'It is more blessed to give than to receive.'"

Bible Verse: Acts 20:35 (NIV)

Joy often comes when we look beyond ourselves and focus on serving others. Jesus taught that it is more blessed to give than to receive, and in giving, we experience the true joy that comes from helping those in need. Serving others reflects God's heart, and as we give our time, resources, and love, we become more like Christ. There is a deep sense of fulfillment and joy when we bless others, and it reminds us that God works through us to bring about His love and care in the world.

When was the last time you experienced joy through serving someone else? Reflect on how giving to others, whether through acts of kindness or practical help, brings you closer to God's heart. How can you find joy in serving others this week?

PRAYER

Father, thank You for the opportunity to serve others. Help me to find joy in giving and serving, knowing that my actions reflect Your love. Open my eyes to those in need, and give me a willing heart to bless others as You have blessed me. Amen.

JOY IN GRATITUDE

"Rejoice always, pray continually, give thanks in all circumstances; for this is God's will for you in Christ Jesus."

Bible Verse: 1 Thessalonians 5:16-18 (NIV)

Gratitude is closely tied to joy. When we choose to give thanks, no matter the circumstances, we open our hearts to joy. Paul encourages us to rejoice always, pray continually, and give thanks in all circumstances. This is not about pretending that everything is perfect but about recognizing God's presence, goodness, and blessings, even in difficult times. Gratitude shifts our focus from what is lacking to what has been given, and this shift leads to greater joy. Thankfulness invites God's peace and joy into our lives.

What are you thankful for today? Reflect on how gratitude can shift your perspective and bring joy, even when circumstances are challenging. How can you cultivate a habit of thanksgiving that leads to a more joyful heart?

PRAYER

Lord, thank You for all that You have blessed me with. Help me to rejoice always and give thanks in all circumstances. May my heart be filled with gratitude, and may Your joy overflow in my life as I focus on Your goodness. Amen.

JOY IN GOD'S PRESENCE

"You make known to me the path of life; you will fill me with joy in your presence, with eternal pleasures at your right hand."

Bible Verse: Psalm 16:11 (NIV)

There is no greater joy than being in the presence of God. The psalmist declares that in God's presence, there is fullness of joy. When we spend time with God through prayer, worship, and meditation on His Word, our hearts are filled with joy that surpasses understanding. This joy is not fleeting or dependent on circumstances; it is rooted in the eternal pleasures of being in a relationship with God. His presence transforms our hearts and brings a deep sense of contentment and peace.

How often do you intentionally seek God's presence? Reflect on how being with God in prayer, worship, or stillness brings true and lasting joy. How can you prioritize time with God to experience the joy of His presence?

PRAYER

Father, thank You for the joy that comes from being in Your presence. I long to experience Your closeness and to be filled with the joy that only You can give. Help me to seek You daily and find my greatest joy in being near to You. In Jesus' name, Amen.

FORGIVENESS

FORGIVING AS GOD FORGIVES

"Be kind and compassionate to one another, forgiving each other, just as in Christ God forgave you."

Bible Verse: Ephesians 4:32 (NIV)

Forgiveness is a cornerstone of Christian life, and it's modeled perfectly in God's forgiveness toward us. In Ephesians, Paul urges us to forgive others "just as in Christ God forgave you." This isn't a suggestion; it's a command rooted in God's grace toward us. When we grasp the magnitude of God's forgiveness—that He has erased every wrong, covered every sin, and welcomed us into His family despite our flaws—it becomes the foundation for extending forgiveness to others. Forgiveness isn't about excusing wrongs or minimizing pain; it's about releasing others from the debt we feel they owe us. In doing so, we mirror the mercy God has shown us, cultivating a heart that's not burdened by bitterness but free to love and heal.

Think of a person or situation that's challenging to forgive. How does remembering God's forgiveness toward you help you release any lingering bitterness?

PRAYER

Lord, thank You for forgiving me fully and freely. Help me to extend that same forgiveness to others, remembering Your mercy and grace. Amen.

THE FREEDOM OF LETTING GO

"For if you forgive other people when they sin against you, your heavenly Father will also forgive you. But if you do not forgive others their sins, your Father will not forgive your sins."

Bible Verse: Matthew 6:14-15 (NIV)

Forgiveness is about freedom, freedom for ourselves and for those we forgive. In the Sermon on the Mount, Jesus connects our willingness to forgive others with God's forgiveness toward us. This isn't about God withholding His love but about the state of our hearts. When we cling to unforgiveness, we close ourselves off from the fullness of God's grace. Holding onto grudges, resentment, and anger becomes a barrier, not only in our relationship with others but also in our relationship with God. By forgiving, we release these heavy burdens and open our hearts to the peace and joy that God offers. Forgiveness is a choice that leads to inner freedom, allowing us to live in harmony with God's will and enjoy His presence more fully.

Consider a hurt or grievance you're carrying. What would it feel like to let go and embrace the freedom that forgiveness brings?

PRAYER

Father, help me to let go of the past and embrace the freedom You offer through forgiveness. May my heart be open to Your grace, allowing Your love to fill every space where anger or hurt once lived. Amen.

FORGIVENESS AND HEALING

"He heals the brokenhearted and binds up their wounds."

Bible Verse: Psalm 147:3 (NIV)

Forgiveness and healing go hand in hand. When we experience hurt, our hearts are often left broken and wounded, and forgiveness becomes part of the healing process. God, the great Healer, is not only capable of mending our physical wounds but also our emotional scars. Forgiveness is one way He brings this healing into our lives. By forgiving, we release the hold that hurt has on us, allowing God to replace pain with peace. The process isn't always immediate; sometimes forgiveness requires time and intentional effort. But as we take steps toward forgiving others, we invite God to restore our hearts fully. This act of surrender can be transformative, changing how we view ourselves, our relationships, and the world around us.

Reflect on an area of hurt in your life. How could choosing to forgive be a step toward deeper healing and wholeness?

PRAYER

Lord, I invite yto heal the places in my heart that have been broken by hurt. Help me to forgive those who have wronged me and trust in your power to restore my soul. Amen.

FORGIVENESS WITHOUT LIMITS

"Then Peter came to Jesus and asked, 'Lord, how many times shall I forgive my brother or sister who sins against me? Up to seven times?' Jesus answered, 'I tell you, not seven times, but seventy-seven times.'"

Bible Verse: Matthew 18:21-22 (NIV)

Forgiveness is limitless. When Peter asked Jesus how many times he should forgive, he thought he was being generous by suggesting seven times. But Jesus' response—seventy-seven times—emphasizes that forgiveness isn't about counting offenses; it's about cultivating a heart that forgives continuously. This radical approach challenges us to move beyond natural human tendencies to keep score or hold grudges. Forgiveness without limits reflects the heart of God, who never tires of forgiving us. It's not easy, but with God's strength, we can forgive repeatedly, knowing that each act of forgiveness brings us closer to His likeness. This kind of relentless forgiveness is a powerful testimony of God's love in us.

Is there someone in your life you've forgiven before but need to forgive again? Ask God for the strength to forgive with a limitless heart.

PRAYER

Jesus, teach me to forgive without limit, as You have forgiven me. Fill my heart with compassion and humility, that I may always reflect Your grace. Amen.

FORGIVENESS AS A PATH TO RECONCILIATION

"All this is from God, who reconciled us to himself through Christ and gave us the ministry of reconciliation."

Bible Verse: 2 Corinthians 5:18 (NIV)

Forgiveness is not only about releasing others from wrongs; it's often the first step toward reconciliation. In 2 Corinthians, Paul speaks of our role in the "ministry of reconciliation," highlighting that forgiveness can restore relationships and bring peace where there was division. True reconciliation is only possible when we forgive with a sincere heart, desiring healing and wholeness. This doesn't mean that every relationship will go back to what it once was, but forgiveness lays the foundation for healthy, respectful connections.

Through forgiveness, we model Christ's love and become agents of peace in a world that often holds onto grudges. We become ambassadors of God's grace, offering the same reconciliation to others that He extended to us.

Is there a relationship in your life that needs reconciliation? How could forgiveness be the first step in rebuilding trust and unity?

PRAYER

Father, help me to be an instrument of reconciliation. Give me the courage to forgive and seek restoration where relationships have been broken. Thank You for the gift of forgiveness and the hope of healing. Amen.

HUMILITY

HUMILITY BEFORE GOD

"Humble yourselves before the Lord, and he will lift you up."

Bible Verse: James 4:10 (NIV)

True humility starts with acknowledging God's greatness and submitting ourselves to Him. James encourages us to humble ourselves before the Lord, promising that in doing so, God will exalt us. This humility is about understanding that we are dependent on God for everything, that all we have and all we are comes from Him. When we recognize God as the source of every blessing and talent, we can approach life with gratitude and humility, trusting that God, not ourselves, is in control.

In what areas of your life do you find it challenging to humble yourself before God? Consider how surrendering control to Him might lead to a greater sense of peace and purpose. Reflect on how acknowledging God's greatness changes your perspective.

PRAYER

Lord, help me to humble myself before You. Let me remember that all I am and all I have is because of Your grace. Teach me to depend on You fully, to recognize Your greatness, and to walk in humility each day. Amen.

HUMILITY WITH OTHERS

"Do nothing out of selfish ambition or vain conceit. Rather, in humility value others above yourselves."

Bible Verse: Philippians 2:3 (NIV)

Humility is not only a posture before God but also a way of relating to others. Paul teaches us to avoid selfish ambition and to value others above ourselves. This doesn't mean belittling ourselves; rather, it is about genuinely considering others' needs and interests. This humble attitude is a reflection of Jesus' own heart. When we put others first, we demonstrate Christ-like love, create unity, and build strong, lasting relationships.

Are there times when pride or self-interest comes between you and others? Reflect on what it means to value others above yourself and how you can demonstrate humility in your relationships. Consider one way you can put others' needs before your own today.

PRAYER

Jesus, give me a humble heart that values others above myself. Help me to serve those around me selflessly, as You did, and let my actions reflect Your love and grace. Amen.

HUMILITY IN SUCCESS

"Let someone else praise you, and not your own mouth; an outsider, and not your own lips."

Bible Verse: Proverbs 27:2 (NIV)

Humility is often tested in times of success. When we achieve something or are praised, it's tempting to seek more recognition or boast about our accomplishments. Proverbs reminds us to let others speak well of us instead of seeking praise ourselves. True humility means being content with quiet success, giving credit to others, and acknowledging God's role in our achievements. Recognizing that all our successes are ultimately God's blessings helps us remain humble and grounded.

How do you handle success and recognition? Think about how you can give God the glory for your achievements and acknowledge the support of those who helped you along the way. What does humble success look like to you?

PRAYER

Father, thank You for every blessing and success. Help me to receive praise with humility, always giving You the glory. May my accomplishments reflect Your grace, and may I honor You in all that I do. Amen.

HUMILITY IN LEARNING AND GROWTH

"When pride comes, then comes disgrace, but with humility comes wisdom."

Bible Verse: Proverbs 11:2 (NIV)

Humility opens the door to growth and wisdom. Proverbs teaches us that pride leads to disgrace, while humility brings wisdom. A humble heart is willing to learn, accepts correction, and grows from mistakes. In contrast, pride resists feedback and refuses to change. Humility allows us to listen, learn, and grow into the people God created us to be, recognizing that we always have room to improve.

Are there areas in your life where pride has kept you from learning or growing? Reflect on the importance of receiving feedback with humility and the value of remaining teachable.

Consider how you can approach challenges or corrections with a humble, open heart.

PRAYER

Lord, grant me a humble heart that is eager to learn and grow. Help me to accept correction graciously and to seek wisdom in all things. May humility guide me as I strive to become more like You. Amen.

HUMILITY IN SERVICE

"Now that I, your Lord and Teacher, have washed your feet, you also should wash one another's feet. I have set you an example that you should do as I have done for you."

Bible Verse: John 13:14-15 (NIV)

Jesus, though Lord and Teacher, took on the role of a servant by washing His disciples' feet, teaching us that true greatness is found in serving others. This act was not just a lesson in humility but a demonstration of love and service. Humility means being willing to serve, regardless of our status or position, and to prioritize the needs of others. In serving, we reflect Christ's humility and show the world His love.

How can you serve those around you with humility? Consider what it means to serve without seeking recognition or reward, simply because it reflects Jesus' love. Think about one act of humble service you can do for someone this week.

PRAYER

Jesus, thank You for showing me what it means to serve in humility. Help me to follow your example, serving others selflessly and with a humble heart. May my actions reveal your love to those around me. Amen.

PATIENCE

PATIENCE IN WAITING ON GOD

"Wait for the Lord; be strong and take heart and wait for the Lord."

Bible Verse: Psalm 27:14 (NIV)

Patience requires trusting in God's timing, even when it doesn't align with our own desires or expectations. David's call to "wait for the Lord" is a reminder that God sees the bigger picture and knows exactly when we need His intervention. Waiting can be challenging, especially when we are eager for answers or solutions. But in those moments of delay, God is often working to strengthen our faith, grow our character, or prepare us for what's ahead. Waiting on God with patience means resting in the assurance that His timing is perfect and that He is faithful to fulfill His promises, even if it takes longer than we would like.

Think about an area of your life where you are waiting for God's answer. Reflect on how patience in this season might be building your faith and shaping your character. What can you do to focus on God's faithfulness as you wait?

PRAYER

Lord, teach me to wait on You with patience and faith. Help me to trust Your timing and to find strength in the waiting. May I always believe that Your plans are good and that You are working for my best, even when I don't see it. Amen.

PATIENCE WITH OTHERS

"Be completely humble and gentle; be patient, bearing with one another in love."

Bible Verse: Ephesians 4:2 (NIV)

Being patient with others is often challenging, particularly when we feel misunderstood, frustrated, or inconvenienced. In Ephesians, Paul encourages us to show humility, gentleness, and patience, bearing with one another in love. Patience with others means giving grace when they fall short, understanding that we, too, need grace and forgiveness. This patience is rooted in love; it's a commitment to see beyond a person's faults and love them as Christ loves us. Instead of reacting out of frustration or impatience, we can choose to respond with understanding, knowing that our patience reflects God's love and mercy in our relationships.

Are there people in your life with whom you struggle to be patient? Reflect on how showing patience in these relationships could reveal Christ's love. Consider one way you can choose to respond with patience rather than frustration today.

PRAYER

Father, help me to be patient and gentle with others, even when it's difficult. Teach me to love others as You love me, bearing with them in patience and kindness. Let my relationships be a testimony of Your love and grace. Amen.

PATIENCE IN TIMES OF SUFFERING

"Be joyful in hope, patient in affliction, faithful in prayer."

Bible Verse: Romans 12:12 (NIV)

Suffering can be one of the greatest tests of patience. In moments of hardship or pain, we often want relief or resolution as quickly as possible. Paul's encouragement to be "patient in affliction" reminds us that God is with us, even in our trials, and that He can use these seasons to strengthen our character and deepen our reliance on Him. Patience in suffering doesn't mean passively enduring pain; it means actively trusting that God is at work and that our struggles have a purpose. This patient endurance helps us grow, giving us a steadfast faith and a closer relationship with God.

Reflect on a time when you faced difficulty and needed to be patient in suffering. How did that experience shape your faith? Consider how you can practice patience in current challenges, trusting that God is using them for your good.

PRAYER

Lord, help me to be patient in times of suffering, trusting that You are with me and that You have a purpose for every trial. Strengthen my faith and give me peace as I endure, knowing that You work all things for good. Amen.

PATIENCE IN PURSUING GOALS AND DREAMS

"Let us not become weary in doing good, for at the proper time we will reap a harvest if we do not give up."

Bible Verse: Galatians 6:9 (NIV)

Achieving our goals or fulfilling dreams often requires long-term commitment and resilience. It can be easy to grow weary or impatient when results don't come as quickly as we hoped. Paul encourages us to keep going, reminding us that we will "reap a harvest" if we stay the course and remain faithful. Patience in our pursuits involves steady work, faith in God's timing, and a commitment to honor Him along the way. By not giving up, we allow God to develop our character, and we position ourselves to receive the blessings He has prepared for us in His perfect time.

Are you feeling discouraged or weary in any areas of your life? Reflect on how staying patient and faithful might lead to eventual rewards. What steps can you take to persevere with patience today?

PRAYER

Lord, give me patience and endurance as I pursue the dreams and goals You have placed in my heart. Help me to trust that Your timing is perfect and that every step I take brings me closer to Your purpose for me. Strengthen me so that I don't give up, even when the journey is long. Amen.

PATIENCE AS A FRUIT OF THE SPIRIT

"Therefore, as God's chosen people, holy and dearly loved, clothe yourselves with compassion, kindness, humility, gentleness, and patience."

Bible Verse: Colossians 3:12 (NIV)

Patience is a core aspect of the Christian life and a fruit of the Spirit. As believers, we are called to "clothe ourselves" in patience, showing it in every interaction and aspect of life. This kind of patience isn't simply a natural disposition; it's a spiritual quality that reflects the work of the Holy Spirit in our lives. When we walk with patience, we reflect Christ's character, bringing peace to those around us and setting an example of steadfast love. Embracing patience as a daily choice strengthens our relationships, our character, and our testimony as followers of Christ.

How does patience reflect Christ's character to those around you? Think about areas in your life where you need to cultivate patience as a fruit of the Spirit. How can you intentionally practice patience today?

PRAYER

Holy Spirit, fill me with Your patience. Help me to "clothe myself" in patience each day, so that my life reflects Your love and peace. May others see Christ in me through my patience, and may my actions honor You in all things. Amen.

FAITHFULNESS

GOD'S FAITHFULNESS TO US

"Because of the Lord's great love we are not consumed, for his compassions never fail. They are new every morning; great is your faithfulness."

Bible Verse: Lamentations 3:22-23 (NIV)

God's faithfulness is unwavering, a bedrock on which we can build our lives. In Lamentations, written during a time of great sorrow and national tragedy, the prophet Jeremiah declares God's faithfulness with profound assurance. Even in the darkest moments, God's love and compassion remain steadfast. His faithfulness is not dependent on our circumstances or our actions; it is a reflection of His unchanging character. Each new day, God renews His mercy toward us, offering fresh hope and strength. Embracing this truth allows us to live with confidence, knowing that no matter what we face, God's faithfulness will carry us through.

How has God shown His faithfulness in your life, even in difficult times? Take a moment to recall specific instances when He provided for you, comforted you, or showed you mercy. Consider how these experiences build your trust in Him.

PRAYER

Lord, thank You for Your faithfulness, which never fails. Help me to remember that Your love and mercy are renewed for me each day. Strengthen my faith so that I may rely on Your promises, even when life is challenging. Amen.

FAITHFULNESS IN SMALL THINGS

"Whoever can be trusted with very little can also be trusted with much, and whoever is dishonest with very little will also be dishonest with much."

Bible Verse: Luke 16:10 (NIV)

Jesus teaches that faithfulness starts with the small, seemingly insignificant tasks. Being faithful in small things may not seem glamorous, but it's in these moments that we demonstrate integrity and build character. Every act of honesty, diligence, and commitment prepares us for greater responsibilities. God honors those who are consistent and trustworthy in the little things, as it shows a heart aligned with His values. This faithfulness builds a strong foundation, making us reliable and trustworthy not only in our work but also in our relationships and spiritual life.

Think about an area in your life where you may need to be more faithful in small things. How can you demonstrate consistency, integrity, or commitment in that area? Consider how these small acts of faithfulness may prepare you for greater responsibilities.

PRAYER

Lord, teach me to be faithful in the small things, knowing that You see every act of diligence and honesty. Help me to build my character with integrity, and let me honor You in every task, no matter how small. Amen.

FAITHFULNESS IN RELATIONSHIPS

"Let love and faithfulness never leave you; bind them around your neck, write them on the tablet of your heart. Then you will win favor and a good name in the sight of God and man."

Bible Verse: Proverbs 3:3-4 (NIV)

Faithfulness in relationships is essential to building trust and deepening bonds with others. Proverbs encourages us to "bind" love and faithfulness to ourselves, letting them define our interactions and decisions. Faithfulness in relationships means being reliable, honest, and supportive through good times and bad. It's about showing up for others, being consistent, and keeping our word. This faithfulness not only blesses those around us but also reflects God's own faithfulness to us. As we practice loyalty and integrity, we mirror the love and reliability that God demonstrates in His relationship with us.

Are there relationships in your life where you could show greater faithfulness? Consider how small acts of consistency, honesty, or encouragement could strengthen these bonds. Reflect on how your faithfulness in relationships can demonstrate God's love to others.

PRAYER

Father, help me to be faithful in my relationships, reflecting Your love and commitment to those I care about. Let my words and actions build trust, and may I honor You through my loyalty and integrity in every connection. Amen.

FAITHFULNESS IN SERVING GOD

"Now it is required that those who have been given a trust must prove faithful."

Bible Verse: 1 Corinthians 4:2 (NIV)

Faithfulness in serving God means honoring the responsibilities, talents, and opportunities He has entrusted to us. As stewards of His gifts, we are called to serve Him with dedication, not seeking recognition or reward, but because we love Him. This kind of faithfulness requires a heart willing to give our best, even when it's not convenient or when no one else is watching. God notices every effort, and He values the consistency of our service. By remaining faithful in what He has given us to do, we show gratitude and reverence for His calling, and we fulfill His purpose for our lives.

Consider how you are using the talents and opportunities God has given you. Are there areas where you could be more faithful in serving Him? Reflect on how consistent, wholehearted service honors God and strengthens your relationship with Him.

PRAYER

Lord, thank You for the gifts and opportunities You have entrusted to me. Help me to serve You faithfully, giving my best in all I do. May my actions bring glory to You, and may I find joy and fulfillment in serving Your purposes. Amen.

THE REWARD OF FAITHFULNESS

"His master replied, 'Well done, good and faithful servant! You have been faithful with a few things; I will put you in charge of many things. Come and share your master's happiness!'"

Bible Verse: Matthew 25:21 (NIV)

In the Parable of the Talents, Jesus tells us the joy that comes from being a "good and faithful servant." Faithfulness brings not only God's approval but also blessings that often exceed our expectations. When we are faithful in what we have been given, God entrusts us with more. This reward is not merely about gaining more responsibility; it's about entering deeper joy and satisfaction in God's presence. Being faithful in all areas of our lives—relationships, work, service, and spiritual growth—leads to a fulfillment that only God can give. The greatest reward is not material; it's the opportunity to share in the joy and love of our Master.

Reflect on how faithfulness has enriched your life. Are there areas where you sense God calling you to greater commitment? Consider the joy and fulfillment that comes from living faithfully and knowing that your efforts please God.

PRAYER

Lord, thank You for the reward that comes with faithfulness. Help me to live in a way that honors You, knowing that my service brings joy to Your heart. May I hear Your words, "Well done, good and faithful servant," as I strive to be faithful in all areas of my life. Amen.

KINDNESS

A KINDNESS THAT LEADS TO CHANGE

"Or do you show contempt for the riches of his kindness, forbearance and patience, not realizing that God's kindness is intended to lead you to repentance?"

Bible Verse: Romans 2:4 (NIV)

God's kindness is not merely a soft gesture; it's a powerful tool He uses to invite us into a closer relationship with Him. Rather than pushing us away or condemning us, God's patient kindness draws us in. It leads us to change because we see that He treats us with a gentle, forgiving love even when we fall short. His kindness is intended to open our hearts, showing us that God's ways are good and trustworthy. When we understand the depth of

God's kindness, it can inspire us to offer the same grace to others, allowing kindness to flow through us.

How has God's kindness changed your life? Reflect on how His kindness inspires you to treat others with compassion, even when it's undeserved.

PRAYER

Lord, thank You for the kindness that draws me closer to You. Teach me to be more like You and share this kindness with others. Amen.

THE CHOICE TO BE KIND

"Be kind and compassionate to one another, forgiving each other, just as in Christ God forgave you."

Bible Verse: Ephesians 4:32 (NIV)

Kindness is often a conscious choice, especially in moments when forgiveness or patience is difficult. When Paul instructs us to be kind and compassionate, he's calling us to go beyond what's easy and model Christ's heart. Choosing kindness over judgment or anger requires humility and empathy. It reminds us that each person carries struggles, and each of us has been forgiven by Christ. Kindness allows us to see others with a softer heart, helping to foster peace and understanding.

In what situations can you choose kindness instead of criticism or frustration? Reflect on how the choice to be kind can bring healing and strength to your relationships.

PRAYER

Father, let kindness guide my responses to others. Help me to forgive as You have forgiven me, and let my actions reflect Your compassion. Amen.

SMALL ACTS, BIG IMPACT

"Those who are kind benefit themselves, but the cruel bring ruin on themselves."

Bible Verse: Proverbs 11:17 (NIV)

Kindness may seem like a simple act, but it holds great power. Proverbs reminds us that being kind blesses not only those around us but also our own lives. Acts of kindness, no matter how small, create a positive impact that ripples outward. When we show kindness, it builds relationships, creates joy, and nurtures a culture of caring. Simple gestures—a kind word, a helping hand—reflect God's love in practical ways and remind people that they are seen and valued. Kindness also brings a sense of purpose and joy to the one giving it, lifting the heart and spirit.

Think of some small ways you can show kindness each day. Reflect on how these actions could make a difference for others and for you.

PRAYER

Lord, fill my heart with a desire to serve others with kindness. Let each small act bring light to those around me and glorify You. Amen.

KINDNESS WHEN IT'S HARD

"Therefore, as God's chosen people, holy and dearly loved, clothe yourselves with compassion, kindness, humility, gentleness and patience."

Bible Verse: Colossians 3:12 (NIV)

It's easy to be kind when things are going well, but showing kindness during stressful or challenging moments reveals true strength. Paul's words remind us to "clothe" ourselves in kindness as a constant part of who we are, regardless of circumstances. When we choose kindness in difficult times, we demonstrate a commitment to God's character, allowing His love to work through us. It's a choice that reveals maturity, self-control, and an understanding that kindness can diffuse conflict and bring peace.

Are there challenging situations where you can show kindness? Reflect on how responding with kindness could bring God's peace to difficult circumstances.

PRAYER

Lord, give me the strength to be kind even in hard times. May my words and actions bring Your love and peace to others. Amen.

KINDNESS WITH A LASTING LEGACY

"Let us not become weary in doing good, for at the proper time we will reap a harvest if we do not give up. Therefore, as we have opportunity, let us do good to all people, especially to those who belong to the family of believers."

Bible Verse: Galatians 6:9-10 (NIV)

Kindness leaves a legacy that endures beyond the moment. Paul's encouragement to keep doing good reminds us that kindness is a seed that grows over time, impacting lives in ways we may never fully see. Even when we're tired, each act of kindness reflects God's love and sows seeds that will bear fruit in time. Whether it's a simple smile or a generous act, kindness builds a legacy of love and compassion that inspires others and strengthens our faith community.

Reflect on how kindness has impacted your life or someone else's. Are there areas where you can sow seeds of kindness and trust that God will use them for good?

PRAYER

Lord, help me to keep sowing seeds of kindness, knowing that You will use them to touch lives in Your time. Give me the endurance to do good without growing weary. Amen.

GENTLENESS

STRENGTH WRAPPED IN GENTLENESS

"Take my yoke upon you and learn from me, for I am gentle and humble in heart, and you will find rest for your souls."

Bible Verse: Matthew 11:29 (NIV)

Jesus describes Himself as "gentle and humble in heart," and this gentleness draws people to Him. Gentleness does not mean weakness or timidity; rather, it reflects a strength that is under control—a deliberate choice to respond with grace and kindness even when firmness is needed. Jesus's gentleness allows others to approach Him without fear, knowing that He will treat them with compassion and understanding. In our own lives, gentleness invites trust and openness in relationships, showing that we value others' feelings and well-being. Gentleness is a strength that helps us respond to conflict, disappointment, and even criticism with a calm spirit, reflecting Christ's heart.

Are there areas in your life where you can respond with more gentleness? Think of how approaching others with a gentle spirit can foster trust and create an atmosphere of peace.

PRAYER

Lord, teach me to embody Your gentleness in my interactions. Help me to be approachable, compassionate, and gentle, even in challenging situations. Amen.

GENTLENESS IN ACTION

"A gentle answer turns away wrath, but a harsh word stirs up anger."

Bible Verse: Proverbs 15:1 (NIV)

The way we respond to others has a powerful impact. Proverbs tells that a gentle response can diffuse tension, while harsh words can fuel conflict. Gentleness is an active choice to remain calm and kind, especially when tempers are high. It allows us to respond to difficult situations without adding more negativity or anger, helping to de-escalate conflicts. Practicing gentleness means choosing our words carefully and taking a moment to respond with understanding, especially when we feel misunderstood or criticized. When we speak with gentleness, we reflect God's wisdom and love, allowing Him to work through us to create peace.

Think about a recent conversation where emotions ran high. How might a gentle response have shifted the tone? Consider how a gentle answer can be a way to show God's love to others.

PRAYER

Father, give me the wisdom to respond with gentleness, especially in tense moments. May my words bring calm and understanding, reflecting Your love to those around me. Amen.

GENTLENESS WITH OURSELVES

"You make your saving help my shield, and your right hand sustains me; your help has made me great."

Bible Verse: Psalm 18:35 (NIV)

We often think of gentleness as something we show to others, but God also calls us to be gentle with ourselves. In Psalm 18, David reflects on how God's gentleness has upheld and strengthened him. Sometimes, we are our harshest critics, holding ourselves to impossible standards or being unforgiving of our mistakes. But God's gentle care reminds us to extend that same grace to ourselves. Being gentle with ourselves doesn't mean excusing sin or failure; it means acknowledging our limitations, accepting God's forgiveness, and growing through His guidance. When we treat ourselves with gentleness, we can approach life with renewed strength and grace.

Are there areas where you're hard on yourself? Reflect on how God's gentleness toward you can inspire you to show grace to yourself, allowing room for growth without harsh self-judgment.

PRAYER

Lord, thank you for your gentle care in my life. Help me to be gentle with myself, accepting your grace and walking in the strength you provide. Amen.

GENTLENESS AS A WITNESS

"But in your hearts revere Christ as Lord. Always be prepared to give an answer to everyone who asks you to give the reason for the hope that you have. But do this with gentleness and respect."

Bible Verse: 1 Peter 3:15 (NIV)

When sharing our faith, Peter encourages us to do so with gentleness and respect. Gentleness shows that we respect the other person's perspective, even if it's different from our own. It's easy to become defensive or forceful when discussing deeply held beliefs, but gentleness demonstrates confidence and compassion. A gentle approach invites others to listen and consider our faith more openly. It shows that we genuinely care for them, not just for winning an argument.

When we witness with gentleness, we reflect the character of Christ and make space for the Holy Spirit to work in others' hearts.

Consider how you share your faith. Are there ways you can approach conversations with more gentleness and respect? Reflect on how this might impact others' willingness to listen.

PRAYER

Lord, help me to share my faith with gentleness and respect, reflecting Your love and inviting others to know You. Let my words and actions be a witness of Your grace. Amen.

GENTLENESS IN LEADERSHIP

"Brothers and sisters, if someone is caught in a sin, you who live by the Spirit should restore that person gently. But watch yourselves, or you also may be tempted."

Bible Verse: Galatians 6:1 (NIV)

Leading with gentleness is a powerful way to support others, especially when correction is needed. Paul's instruction to "restore gently" reflects an approach that values the person over the problem. When we gently guide others, we show respect for their dignity and create a safe space for growth. Gentle leadership seeks to restore rather than condemn, offering understanding and encouragement. This requires humility, patience, and empathy, recognizing that we all need grace. Gentleness in leadership fosters trust and openness, encouraging others to learn and grow without fear of harsh judgment.

Think of someone you are guiding or helping. How might a gentle approach create a more supportive environment for their growth? Reflect on how leading with gentleness honors God and builds up others.

PRAYER

Father, give me a heart of gentleness in leadership. Let my guidance be a reflection of your patience and love, inspiring growth and restoration in those I lead. Amen.

GRATITUDE

A HEART OF THANKSGIVING

"Give thanks in all circumstances; for this is God's will for you in Christ Jesus."

Bible Verse: 1 Thessalonians 5:18 (NIV)

Gratitude is central to our faith because it shifts our focus from what we lack to the abundance God has already provided. Paul's words in 1 Thessalonians remind us to be thankful not just for the good times but in all circumstances. This doesn't mean that we must be thankful for every hardship but rather that we find reasons to thank God even amid challenges. When we embrace gratitude, we recognize God's constant presence and provision, whether life is easy or difficult. Gratitude is an act of trust that God is working for our good, even when we can't see the full picture. As we give thanks, our hearts align with His will, and we're reminded of His unchanging faithfulness.

Reflect on areas of your life where gratitude feels challenging. Consider how practicing gratitude in those moments could deepen your faith and bring you peace.

PRAYER

Lord, help me cultivate a heart of thanksgiving. Teach me to trust You in all circumstances, knowing that Your love surrounds me always. Amen.

COUNTING EVERY BLESSING

"Praise the Lord, my soul, and forget not all his benefits."

Bible Verse: Psalm 103:2 (NIV)

Gratitude requires intentionality. The psalmist urges us not to "forget" the Lord's blessings, emphasizing the importance of recalling specific ways God has blessed us. When life gets busy, we can overlook small blessings or take God's goodness for granted. Making a habit of counting our blessings—even small things like a warm meal, a friend's smile, or the beauty of nature—reminds us of God's love and provision in every detail. Each blessing, big or small, is evidence of God's kindness and care. By taking time to reflect on these blessings, we develop a grateful heart that honors Him and fills us with joy.

Take a moment to list three blessings in your life today. How does focusing on these blessings affect your mood and perspective?

PRAYER

Heavenly Father, open my eyes to see your blessings all around me. May I never take your goodness for granted, but always give thanks for each gift you provide. Amen.

GRATITUDE DURING TRIALS

"Consider it pure joy, my brothers and sisters, whenever you face trials of many kinds, because you know that the testing of your faith produces perseverance."

Bible Verse: James 1:2-3 (NIV)

It may seem counterintuitive, but gratitude is possible even during trials. James encourages us to see trials as opportunities for growth, where God refines and strengthens our faith. This mindset requires us to look beyond immediate discomfort and to trust that God is using each challenge for our good. When we express gratitude amid hardship, we acknowledge that God is greater than our struggles and that He is actively working in us to bring about something beautiful. Such gratitude deepens our resilience, encourages our hearts, and helps us see challenges through a lens of hope. It's a reminder that God's plans for us are always rooted in His love and wisdom.

Consider a trial you're currently facing. How might you reframe it as an opportunity for growth, thanking God for the lessons He is teaching you?

PRAYER

Lord, even in difficult times, I choose to trust and thank You. Help me to see trials as opportunities to grow closer to You, and strengthen my faith in Your perfect plan. Amen.

GRATITUDE AS WORSHIP

"Let the message of Christ dwell among you richly as you teach and admonish one another with all wisdom through psalms, hymns, and songs from the Spirit, singing to God with gratitude in your hearts."

Bible Verse: Colossians 3:16 (NIV)

Gratitude is a profound form of worship. When we praise God with thankful hearts, we honor Him for who He is and for all He has done. Worship that flows from gratitude is a powerful way to draw close to God, to remember His promises, and to invite His presence into our lives. Singing with gratitude, as Paul describes, is a declaration of God's goodness that uplifts our spirit and reminds us of His constant care. In times of joy and sorrow alike, worship can become an anchor for our souls, transforming our gratitude into an outpouring of love and adoration for God.

How does expressing gratitude through worship impact your relationship with God? Take a few minutes to thank Him for specific ways He's been present in your life.

PRAYER

Father, let my heart overflow with gratitude as I worship You. May my songs of praise remind me of Your goodness and draw me closer to You. Amen.

GRATITUDE THAT LEADS TO GENEROSITY

"You will be enriched in every way so that you can be generous on every occasion, and through us your generosity will result in thanksgiving to God."

Bible Verse: 2 Corinthians 9:11 (NIV)

A grateful heart naturally overflows into generosity. Paul teaches that when we recognize how God has enriched us—spiritually, emotionally, or materially—we are moved to bless others in return. Gratitude opens our eyes to the abundance of God's provision, shifting our focus from scarcity to sufficiency. When we give out of gratitude, our generosity becomes an extension of our thankfulness to God. This cycle of blessing and thanksgiving allows us to be a reflection of

God's love and generosity, creating a ripple effect of gratitude in our communities. Generosity rooted in gratitude not only blesses others but glorifies God as the source of all good things.

Think of a way you can be generous this week as an expression of gratitude. Consider how your gift might point others toward God's love and provision.

PRAYER

Lord, thank You for all you've given me. Help me to live with an open and generous heart so that others may experience your love through my gratitude. Amen.

TRUST

TRUSTING BEYOND UNDERSTANDING

"Trust in the Lord with all your heart and lean not on your own understanding; in all your ways submit to him, and he will make your paths straight."

Bible Verse: Proverbs 3:5-6 (NIV)

Trusting in God with our whole heart often means surrendering our desire to understand everything. This can be challenging because human nature craves clarity and control, yet God calls us to trust beyond what we can see or grasp. Proverbs 3 reminds us that real trust involves letting go of our limited perspectives and acknowledging that God's wisdom far surpasses our own. When we lean on our understanding, we may misinterpret circumstances or doubt God's guidance, but when we trust Him fully, we allow Him to direct our lives and align our paths with His perfect plan. Trust is not passive; it's an active choice to submit our fears, uncertainties, and plans into God's hands, believing that He is good and faithful. Even when life doesn't make sense, God promises to straighten our paths, bringing clarity in His timing. This kind of trust is transformative, helping us to walk in peace and confidence that God is in control.

What areas of your life are you still trying to control? How can you practice trusting God beyond your understanding today?

PRAYER

Lord, help me to trust you wholeheartedly. Give me the faith to surrender my understanding and believe that your ways are higher. Lead me in your path, and guide my steps each day. Amen.

A TRUST THAT GROWS IN TRIALS

"Consider it pure joy, my brothers and sisters, whenever you face trials of many kinds because you know that the testing of your faith produces perseverance."

Bible Verse: James 1:2-3 (NIV)

Trust is often strengthened in the face of difficulty. When we experience trials, we may be tempted to question God's goodness or wonder why we are facing challenges. But James encourages us to see trials as opportunities for growth, where our trust in God can deepen. Through life's difficulties, we learn to rely on God more completely and discover that He is faithful, even in hardship. Trials reveal our dependence on God, showing us that we cannot rely solely on ourselves. They push us to grow in endurance and mature our faith. It's in these moments that we find God's presence most vividly as we lean on Him for strength and comfort. Trust developed in trials is robust, enduring the storms of life and becoming a testimony to others of God's unchanging faithfulness.

Reflect on a recent trial or challenge. How did it impact your trust in God? In what ways can trials serve as stepping stones to deepen your faith?

PRAYER

Father, thank You for Your presence in my trials. Strengthen my trust in You as I face challenges, and help me to grow in faith through every difficulty. May I find joy in knowing that You are working in me, even in hard times. Amen.

TRUSTING GOD'S TIMING

"He has made everything beautiful in its time. He has also set eternity in the human heart, yet no one can fathom what God has done from beginning to end."

Bible Verse: Ecclesiastes 3:11 (NIV)

Trusting God's timing can be one of the most difficult aspects of faith. We live in a fast-paced world that encourages instant gratification, but God's timing operates differently, often requiring us to wait and trust His wisdom. Ecclesiastes reminds us that God's plans are beautifully timed, even when we may not see the full picture. While waiting, we may experience frustration or doubt, but these seasons can also be profound times of growth. Trusting in His timing builds patience and teaches us to rely on God's wisdom over our own. God's delays are not denials; rather, they are moments when He is orchestrating the best for us in ways we may not understand. By trusting His timing, we align our hearts with His purposes, surrendering our desire to rush the process and embracing His perfect plan.

Is there an area of your life where you are struggling to wait on God's timing? How can you shift your perspective to see waiting as a time of growth?

PRAYER

Lord, I surrender my impatience and my desire for quick answers. Help me to trust in Your timing, knowing that You make everything beautiful in its time. Teach me to wait with faith, believing that You are working all things together for good. Amen.

TRUST IN GOD'S PROVISION

"And my God will meet all your needs according to the riches of his glory in Christ Jesus."

Bible Verse: Philippians 4:19 (NIV)

God's provision is a foundation of trust, reminding us that He knows our needs and provides for us abundantly. Philippians 4:19 assures us that God is more than capable of meeting our needs through His boundless riches in Christ. This promise encourages us not to rely on material wealth, job security, or human sources alone but to place our confidence in God as our provider. Trusting in His provision helps us live with a sense of peace, even when resources appear limited or uncertain. Sometimes, God provides in ways we don't expect, teaching us that His resources are limitless and that His care for us is unwavering. Trusting in God's provision means recognizing that our true security and well-being rest in Him. When we focus on His faithfulness, we find freedom from worry, knowing that He will provide everything we need.

Consider a time when God provided for you unexpectedly. How can you hold onto that memory to strengthen your trust in His provision today?

PRAYER

Heavenly Father, thank You for being my provider. Help me to trust that You will meet my needs and provide for me in ways that go beyond what I can imagine. Teach me to rest in Your abundance and to live without fear. Amen.

WALKING IN TRUST AMIDST UNCERTAINTY

"So do not fear, for I am with you; do not be dismayed, for I am your God. I will strengthen you and help you; I will uphold you with my righteous right hand."

Bible Verse: Isaiah 41:10 (NIV)

In times of uncertainty, God calls us to trust Him wholeheartedly. Isaiah 41:10 is a powerful reminder of His presence and support, especially when life feels overwhelming or unclear. This verse speaks to God's commitment to strengthen, help, and uphold us, even when we face situations beyond our control. Trusting God amid uncertainty is a declaration of faith that He is bigger than our fears and more stable than our circumstances. It's a choice to believe that He is actively working, guiding, and protecting us. When we hold onto God's promises, we find peace and assurance, knowing that we are not walking through life alone. This trust helps us navigate life's unpredictability with a confident heart, resting in the One who holds our future.

Are there areas of your life where you feel uncertain or afraid? How can you practice trusting in God's presence and promises in these areas?

PRAYER

God, in times of uncertainty, help me to remember that You are with me. Strengthen my trust, and remind me that I am upheld by Your righteous right hand. May I walk forward in faith, confident in Your love and care. Amen.

www.ingramcontent.com/pod-product-compliance
Lightning Source LLC
LaVergne TN
LVHW010200070526
838199LV00062B/4432